5-Minute French

Berlitz Publishing

New York   London   Singapore

5-MINUTE FRENCH

Contacting the Editors
Every effort has been made to provide accurate information in this publication, but changes are inevitable. The publisher cannot be responsible for any resulting loss, inconvenience or injury. We would appreciate it if readers would call our attention to any errors or outdated information by contacting us at: comments@ berlitzpublishing.com

Fifth Printing: November 2013
Printed in China
ISBN 978-981-268-4578

Senior Commissioning Editor: Kate Drynan
Cover Design: Claudia Petrilli
Interior Design, Composition and Editorial: Booklinks Publishing Services
Production Manager: Vicky Glover
Cover: © iStockphoto.com/Dale Taylor

Contents

Contents

How to Use This Book

By using *5-Minute French* every day, you can start speaking French in just minutes. The 5-Minute program introduces you to a new language and gets you speaking right away. Take a few minutes before or after work, before you go to sleep at night or any time that feels right to work on one lesson a day. If you want, you can even go ahead and do two lessons a day. Just have fun while you learn; you'll be speaking French in no time.

- The book is divided into 99 lessons. Each provides a bite-sized learning opportunity that you can complete in minutes.

- Each unit has 8 lessons presenting important vocabulary, phrases and other information needed in everyday French.

- A review at the end of each unit provides an opportunity to test your knowledge before you move on.

- Unless otherwise noted, *5-Minute French* uses formal language. In everyday French, the formal is usually used between adults who are not close friends or family and in professional settings. The informal is used with familiar friends and family and when addressing children.

Bonjour !

- Real life language and activities introduce the vocabulary, phrases and grammar covered in the lessons that follow. You'll see dialogues, postcards, e-mails and other everyday correspondence in French.

- You can listen to the dialogues, articles, e-mails and other presentations on the *5-Minute French* audio CD.

 5-Minute French audio
When you see this symbol , you'll know to listen to the specified track on the *5-Minute French* audio CD.

Smart Phrases

- In these lessons you'll find useful everyday phrases. You can listen to these phrases on the audio program.

- Extra Phrases enrich your knowledge and understanding of everyday French. These are not practiced in the activities, but they're there for those who want to learn.

SMART TIP

Boxes like these are here to extend your French knowledge. You'll find differences in French from country to country, extra language conventions and other helpful information on how to speak better French.

Words to Know

- Core Words are important words related to the lesson topic. In some lessons these words are divided into sub-categories. You can listen to these words on our audio program.

- Extra Words are other helpful words to know.

Smart Grammar

- Don't let the name scare you. Smart Grammar covers the basic parts of speech you'll need to know if you want to speak French easily and fluently.

- From verb usage to forming questions, the 5-Minute program provides quick and easy explanations and examples for how to use these structures.

CULTURE TIP

Boxes like these introduce useful cultural information about French-speaking countries.

Unit Review Here you'll have a chance to practice what you've learned.

Challenge
Extend your knowledge even further with a challenge activity.

SMART PRONUNCIATION

Boxes like these demonstrate specific pronunciation tools. For example, did you know that the final consonants of most French words are not pronounced? You'll learn more as you move further along in the book.

Internet Activity

- Internet activities take you to **www.berlitzbooks.com/5minute**, where you can test drive your new language skills. Just look for the computer symbol.

This section is designed to make you familiar with the sounds of French using our simplified phonetic transcription. You'll find the pronunciation of the French letters and sounds explained below, together with their "imitated" equivalents. Simply read the pronunciation as if it were English, noting any special rules below.

In French, all syllables are pronounced the same, with no extra stress on any particular syllable. French contains nasal vowels, which are indicated in the pronunciation by a vowel followed by an N. This N should not be pronounced strongly, but it is there to show the nasal quality of the previous vowel. A nasal vowel is pronounced simultaneously through the mouth and the nose.

Although the final consonants of most words are not pronounced in French, when a word with a final consonant comes before a word beginning with a vowel, the two pronunciations often run together. In this case the final consonant is pronounced as if it begins the following word.

Consonants

Letter	Approximate Pronunciation	Example	Pronunciation
cc	1. before e, i, like cc in accident	accessible	ahk·seh·seebl
	2. elsewhere, like cc in accommodate	d'accord	dah·kohr
ch	like sh in shut	chercher	shehr·shay
ç	like s in sit	ça	sah
g	1. before e, i, y, like s in pleasure	manger	mawN·zhay
	2. before a, o, u, like g in go	garçon	gahr·sohN
h	always silent	homme	ohm
j	like s in pleasure	jamais	zhah·may
qu	like k in kill	qui	kee
r	rolled in the back of the mouth, like gargling	rouge	roozh
w	usually like v in voice	wagon	vah·gohN

b, c, d, f, k, l, m, n, p, s, t, v, x and z are pronounced as in English.

Vowels

Letter	Approximate Pronunciation	Example	Pronunciation
a, à, â	between the a in hat and the a in father	**mari**	mah·ree
e	sometimes like a in about	**je**	zhuh
è, ê, e	like e in get	**même**	mehm
é, ez	like a in late	**été**	ay·tay
i	like ee in meet	**il**	eel
o, ô	generally like o in roll	**donner**	doh·nay
u	like ew in dew	**une**	ewn

Sounds spelled with two or more letters

Letter	Approximate Pronunciation	Example	Pronunciation
ai, ay, aient, ais, ait, aî, ei	like a in late	**j'ai** **vais**	zhay vay
ai, ay, aient, ais, ait, aî, ei	like e in get	**chaîne** **peine**	shehn pehn
(e)au	similar to o	**chaud**	shoh
eu, eû, œu	like u in fur but short like a puff of air	**euro**	uh·roh
euil, euille	like uh + y	**feuille**	fuhy
ail, aille	like ie in tie	**taille**	tie
ille	1. like ee in see followed by u in cut 2. like eel	**famille** **ville**	fah·meey veel
oi, oy	like w followed by the a in hat	**moi**	mwah
ou, oû	like o in move or oo in hoot	**nouveau**	noo·voh
ui	approximately like wee in between	**traduire**	trah·dweer

In this unit you will:

- learn common phrases to greet and say goodbye.
- say your name and where you are from.
- learn personal pronouns and the verb *être* (to be).
- learn common phrases and words about your nationality.

LESSON
1

Bonjour !

Dialogue

Martine meets her new neighbor Pierre. Listen as she introduces herself and asks Pierre where he is from.

Martine Bonjour. Je m'appelle Martine. Comment vous appelez-vous ?

Pierre Je m'appelle Pierre. Enchanté.

Martine Je suis française. Et vous, d'où venez-vous ?

Pierre Je suis belge.

Martine Enchantée, Pierre.

Pierre Également. Au revoir.

> **SMART TIP**
>
> When talking about nationalities, a French speaker might describe himself or herself as a person of a particular country, *Je suis français/française* (I am French (m/f)), or say where he or she comes from, *Je viens de France* (I come from France). It is less common to use—as we do in English—the verb "to be" with a country of origin: *Je suis de France* (I am from France).

Activity A

Circle **T** for true and **F** for false.

1 This meeting happens during the day.   **T / F**
2 Pierre is happy to meet Martine.   **T / F**
3 Martine is from Switzerland.   **T / F**
4 Pierre is from Belgium.   **T / F**

Activity B

Fill in the missing questions or statements with phrases from the dialogue.

Je m'appelle Martine. _____ ?

Je m'appelle Pierre. _____.

Je suis française. Et vous, _____ ?

Je suis _____.

> **CULTURE TIP**
>
> In France friends and family members often greet each other with a kiss called *le bisou* or *la bise*. They typically give two kisses, one on each cheek, but this depends on the region. In Provence they might give three kisses, while in Nantes they might give four.

Core Phrases

À bientôt.	See you soon.
Au revoir !	Goodbye!
Bon après-midi.	Good afternoon.
Bonjour.	Good morning.
Bonjour !	Hello!
Bonne nuit.	Good night. (at bedtime)
Bonsoir.	Good evening/Good night. (when meeting or parting)
Comment vous appelez-vous ?	What is your name?
D'où venez-vous ?	Where are you from?

Extra Phrases

Bien, merci.	Fine, thank you.
Ça va ?	How are you?
Ça va.	I'm fine.
Également.	Likewise.
Enchanté/Enchantée.	Nice to meet you. (m/f)
Je m'appelle ___.	My name is ___.

Activity A

What do you say if you want to...

1   ...say hello?

_____

2   ...ask someone his/her name?

_____

3   ...ask someone where he/she is from?

_____

4   ...say goodbye?

_____

Activity B

For each picture write the appropriate French greeting: *Bonjour, Bonsoir* or *Bonne nuit*.

1   _____

2   _____

3   _____

Words to Know

l'Amérique du Nord
North America

Core Words

la Belgique		Belgium
le Canada		Canada
les États-Unis		United States
la France		France
le Royaume-Uni		United Kingdom
le Sénégal		Senegal

Activity A

Write the corresponding number on the maps for each country.

1   la France
2   le Sénégal
3   les États-Unis
4   la Belgique
5   le Royaume-Uni

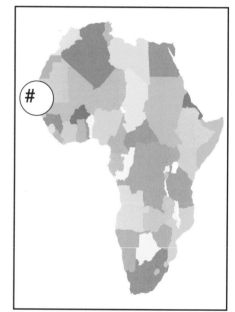

l'Afrique
Africa

l'Europe
Europe

Activity B

Match each flag to the name of the country.

1   le Canada
2   la Belgique
3   la France
4   le Royaume-Uni

Smart Grammar

Personal Pronouns

je	I
tu	you (sing., inf.)
il/elle	he/she
nous	we
vous	you (pl. or sing., form.)
ils/elles	they (m/f)

Abbreviations

masculine	m	singular	sing.	informal	inf.
feminine	f	plural	pl.	formal	form.

Activity A

Write the correct singular pronoun under each picture.

1 _____
I

2 _____
she

3 _____
he

4 _____
you (inf.)

Activity B

Write the correct plural pronoun under each picture.

1 _____
they

2 _____
they

3 _____
we

4 _____
we

Activity C

Write the pronoun you use when talking about…

1 …yourself. _____

2 …a woman. _____

3 …a man. _____

4 …a group of women. _____

5 …a group of men. _____

SMART TIPS

- Use the masculine plural pronoun if there is at least one male in the group.

- When you first meet someone, address him or her as *vous* until you are told it is OK to use *tu*. When addressing a group of people, elders or in formal situations, use *vous*.

- The personal pronoun *on* is generally used as the equivalent of the English "one," as in the phrase "One should always be on time." It is conjugated the same as *il/elle*.

LESSON 5

D'où venez-vous ?

Les langues et les nationalités

Le français est la langue officielle de trente pays, comme la France, le Canada, la Belgique, la Suisse, Haïti et le Cameroun. Le français est aussi une langue non-officielle dans d'autres pays comme le Maroc et l'Algérie. Le tableau vous donne des exemples de pays, de nationalités et de langues.

Pays	Nationalité	Langue
la Belgique	belge	français, néerlandais, allemand
le Cameroun	camerounais/ camerounaise (m/f)	français, anglais
le Canada	canadien/ canadienne (m/f)	français, anglais
la France	français/ française (m/f)	français
Haïti	haïtien/haïtienne (m/f)	français, créole
la Suisse	suisse	français, italien, allemand, romanche

Language and Nationality

French is the official language of 30 countries, like France, Canada, Belgium, Switzerland, Haiti and Cameroon. French is also spoken as an unofficial language in countries like Morocco and Algeria. The table gives you some other examples of countries, nationalities and languages.

Where Are You From?

Read the article about French-speaking countries and nationalities. Underline the French words that are familiar or similar to any words in English. Then read the English translation.

Activity A

Complete the bilingual chart with words from the article. The first one is done for you.

country	pays
language	
nationality	
French	
English	

Activity B

Look at the French article and table, then circle the correct answer.

1 Someone from Canada is

   a anglais/anglaise   **b canadien/canadienne**

2 Someone from Belgium is

   a belge   **b français/française**

3 People in Haiti speak

   a haïtien   **b français**

4 French is the official language in 30

   a pays   **b langues**

SMART TIP

Words for nationality and languages are not capitalized in French unless they are at the beginning of a sentence. For example, in English we write: "I am French. I speak French." In French, this is: *Je suis français. Je parle français.* The only other time you capitalize a nationality is when you use it as a noun. In English, we say "the Belgians." In French, *les Belges.*

Words to Know

Core Words

américain/américaine	American (m/f)
anglais/anglaise	English (m/f)
australien/australienne	Australian (m/f)
canadien/canadienne	Canadian (m/f)
espagnol/espagnole	Spanish (m/f)
français/française	French (m/f)
suisse	Swiss

Extra Words

allemand/allemande	German (m/f)
belge	Belgian
portugais/portugaise	Portuguese (m/f)
irlandais/irlandaise	Irish (m/f)
italien/italienne	Italian (m/f)

Activity A

Choose the correct nationality for each person.

 1 (French) Hélène est _____.
                   belge/française

 2 (American) Sarah est _____.
                   américaine/anglaise

 3 (English) Tim est _____.
                   anglais/canadien

 4 (Australian) Matthew est _____.
                   irlandais/australien

Activity B

Use the vocabulary from the word box to identify each dish's nationality.

> canadienne   anglaise   française
> américaine   espagnole

 1 _____

 2 _____

 3 _____

 4 _____

 5 _____

SMART TIP

In Activity B, the feminine forms *anglaise, espagnole* and *américaine* are used because you were identifying the food's *nationalité* (nationality). Remember that *nationalité* is a feminine noun, so the adjective used takes the feminine form. Even if we are talking about a man's *nationalité*, the feminine form must be used.

LESSON 7

Smart Phrases

Core Phrases

Vous êtes anglais/anglaise ?	Are you English?
Je suis canadien.	I'm Canadian.
Parlez-vous français ?	Do you speak French?
Un peu.	A little.
Je parle bien/mal.	I speak well/poorly.

Activity A

What do you say if you want to…

1   …ask someone if he/she is French? _____

2   …say you speak a language well? _____

3   …say you speak a little? _____

Your Turn

Imagine you just met someone while traveling in France. Use the phrases and vocabulary you've learned to create a dialogue. Ask about the person's nationality and the language he/she speaks. Write your questions in the You column. Write the answers in the Person from France column.

You	Person from France
Q1	A1
Q2	A2

LESSON 8

Smart Grammar

The verb *être* (to be)

The verb *être* has several uses, including:

- introducing yourself or a person
- telling a person's nationality

Singular

je	suis	I am
tu	es	you are
il/elle	est	he/she is

Examples

Je suis Lisa.	I am Lisa.
C'est André.	He is André.

Activity A

Fill in the blanks with the correct form of the verb *être*.

1. Je _____ Julien.

2. Tu _____ canadien/canadienne ?

3. _____-tu français/française ?

4. C'_____ Marie.

SMART TIP

In French, questions can be formed in two ways: with a rising intonation at the end of a statement, as in *Vous êtes américain ?*, or by inverting the verb and pronoun, like in *Êtes-vous américain ?* Both constructions are acceptable in written and oral French.

Plural

nous	sommes	we are
vous	êtes	you are
ils/elles	sont	they are

Examples

Nous sommes français.	We are French.
Vous êtes suisse.	You are Swiss.

Activity B

Fill in the blanks with the correct form of the verb *être*.

1. Vous _____ américain(s)/américaine(s).

2. Nous _____ suisses.

3. Ils _____ allemands.

4. Elles _____ portugaises.

Your Turn

Eve, Didier and Pauline are getting to know each other. Complete their conversation with the correct form of the verb *être*.

Didier (to Eve)
D'où venez-vous ? Vous _____ canadienne ?

Eve (to Didier and Pauline)
Non, je viens du Royaume-Uni. Je _____ anglaise. Et vous, vous _____ français ?

Didier Je _____ français et Pauline _____ suisse.

Activity A

Complete the following chart.

Nom	Pays	Nationalité
Madeleine		française
Paul	la Belgique	
Claire		canadienne
Brian	les États-Unis	
Katie		anglaise

Activity B

Using the verb *être*, write a complete sentence saying each person's nationality.

Example Pauline, le Royaume-Uni: Pauline est anglaise.

1 tu, les États-Unis:

_____

2 Lisa, l'Espagne:

_____

3 vous, le Canada:

_____

4 Emile, la France:

_____

Activity C

Alex is visiting France. Complete the dialogue as he speaks with his *guide touristique* (tour guide).

Guide _____ ! Bienvenue en France !

Alex Bonjour ! _____ Alex Cromwell.
Et vous, _____ ?

Guide _____ Marc. Enchanté.

Alex Enchanté. _____ français ?

Guide Oui. _____ ?

Alex _____ des États-Unis. _____ anglais ?

Guide Un peu.

Alex Je parle _____ et _____.

Guide Bien !

Alex _____, Marc.

Guide Au revoir !

Activity D

Find the countries and the nationalities from the box in the word search. They may be written forward, backwards, upside down or diagonally.

> Canada France anglais États-Unis
> français Sénégal canadienne

```
L  E  S  É  T  A  T  S  U  N  I  S  S  S  O  S
É  Y  P  I  O  S  E  É  N  Ç  N  A  I  É  L  B
N  A  A  T  L  C  S  N  A  N  A  D  A  N  A  C
A  D  A  N  N  C  A  É  U  D  P  O  L  É  A  B
C  A  N  A  D  I  E  N  N  E  P  C  G  G  E  E
Á  U  R  A  N  A  D  É  E  N  S  E  N  A  H  L
E  F  R  A  N  Ç  A  I  S  G  N  W  A  L  U  G
B  E  L  G  I  Q  U  E  N  E  Q  O  S  Á  D  E
```

Challenge

Can you find the French for *Belgium* and *Belgian* in the word search? Write them below.

Belgium _____

Belgian _____

Activity E

Correct the error in each sentence. Write the correct version of the sentence on the line provided.

1 Au revoir ! Je m'appelle Laure. _____

2 Nous sont du Canada. _____

3 Corinne est de la Belgique. Corinne est française.

_____

4 Marc est américaine. _____

5 Je parle suisse. _____

6 Annie est canadien. _____

Internet Activity

Are you interested in learning more French names? Go to **www.berlitzbooks.com/5minute** for a list of sites with French names. Browse and pick three or four names you like. Practice saying those names aloud. Then try putting *Je m'appelle…* in front of each one.

In this unit you will:
- use vocabulary for people, animals, things and numbers 1–30.
- learn the differences between masculine and feminine, and singular and plural nouns.
- use the definite articles and regular –er and –ir verbs.
- practice filling in a form with basic information about yourself.
- learn how to ask for a telephone number and an address.

LESSON 1

La carte postale

A Postcard from France

Look at the front and back of *la carte postale* (the postcard). Read the text, then circle the words that name people, things or animals.

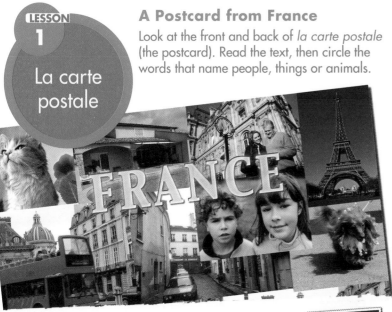

Chère Hélène,

I'm having a great time in Paris, and I'm finally learning some French. Look at the picture! **Regarde la photo ! Regarde les animaux. Regarde les chats et les chiens. Regarde les gens ! Regarde les garçons, les filles, les hommes et les femmes.** *This is a very nice place. I like* **les maisons** *and* **les immeubles** *very much.* **Regarde les voitures et les autobus.** *They are so colorful! This photo shows you* **les personnes, les animaux et les choses** *I'm seeing.*

I miss you. **Tu me manques.**

PS: How's my **français ?**

Robert

Ms. Hélène Seurat
Box 219
Anaheim, California
U. S. A.

Activity A

Circle **T** for true and **F** for false.

1 Robert is visiting France.   T / F
2 Robert's postcard describes mountains and rivers.   T / F
3 Robert likes the houses and buildings.   T / F
4 The postcard describes colorful cars and buses.   T / F

Activity B

Write the French words that name…

1 …people in the postcard.

personnes

2 …things in the postcard.

choses

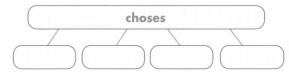

3 …animals in the postcard.

animaux

Extension Activity

If you know more words for people, animals and things add them to the word webs above.

SMART TIP

Notice how the words for people, animals and things in the postcard end with an –s, –es or –aux. This is because they are in the plural form. The singular forms of the words are: *chat, chien, garçon, fille, homme, femme, maison, immeuble* and *voiture.*

Core Words

la fille	le garçon	l'homme	la femme
girl	boy	man (m)	woman

l'oiseau	le chat	le chien
bird (m)	cat	dog

l'autobus	la voiture
bus (m)	car

la rue	la maison	l'immeuble
street	house	building (m)

Activity A
Write the French word for each item in the pictures.

1

2

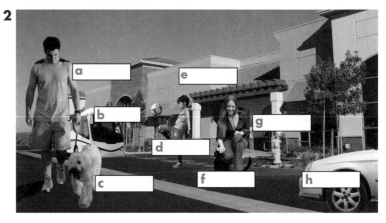

Activity B
Write *féminin* (feminine) or *masculin* (masculine) to classify each noun.

1 chien   _____

2 garçon   _____

3 voiture   _____

4 rue   _____

5 immeuble   _____

6 maison   _____

7 chat   _____

8 autobus   _____

Smart Phrases

Core Phrases

Regarde les gens !   Look at the people!
Regarde les animaux !   Look at the animals!
Cher/Chère _____.   Dear _____. (m/f)
Je m'amuse bien.   I am having a great time.
Tu me manques.   I miss you.

Activity A

Laure is walking with Emile. As they walk, she points at people and
things. Write a phrase in each speech balloon to indicate what
Laure shows Emile.

1 _____
_____

2 _____
_____

Activity B

Fill in the blanks to help
Laure write a postcard
to her friend.

_____ Elaine,

Je m'amuse bien ici, et j'apprends (un peu)

de _____. _____ les gens !

Regarde les _____ ! Regarde

le _____ ! _____ les animaux !

Tu me _____.

Laure

Ms. Hélène Seurat
Box 219
Anaheim, California
U. S. A.

LESSON 4
Smart Grammar

Singular and Plural Nouns

To form a plural noun in French, you generally add –s to the end of the word. However, there are exceptions:

- When the singular noun ends in –s, –x or –z in the masculine form, add nothing: *le nez* (nose)/*les nez* (noses).

- If the noun ends in –eu or –eau, add –x: *l'oiseau/les oiseaux*.

- If a masculine singular noun ends in –ail or –al, add –aux: *l'animal/les animaux*.

- There are some nouns that end in –ou that take –x in the plural form rather than –s: *le genou* (knee)/*les genoux* (knees).

Activity A

Write the plural form of the nouns.

1 homme _____

2 sac  _____

3 crayon  _____

4 oiseau _____

> **SMART TIP**
>
> When a noun begins with a vowel, *le* and *la* are shortened to *l'*. Instead of saying *le animal*, you say *l'animal*. In this case, try to decipher the gender of the word from the spelling.

Definite Articles

The definite article (the) in French varies with the gender and number of the noun.

le (m, sing.)
la (f, sing.)
les (m/f, pl.)

Activity B

Write the correct definite article next to each noun.

1 _____ garçon
2 _____ rue
3 _____ chiens
4 _____ femmes
5 _____ fille
6 _____ autobus

Activity C

Look at the pictures and write the corresponding nouns with the correct definite articles.

1 _____

2 _____

3 _____

4 _____

Your Turn

See if you can guess the article of these nouns.

1 ___ porte (door)
2 ___ lettres (letters)
3 ___ papier (paper)
4 ___ bateau (ship)
5 ___ poubelle (trash can)

20 **Unit 2** Nouns and Numbers

CARTE DE DÉBARQUEMENT
ne concerne pas les voyageurs de nationalité francaise
ni les ressortissants des autres pays membres de la C.E.E.

Nom:	Jameson
Prénom(s):	Jennifer K.
Sexe: F	**Date de naissance:** jour: 30 mois: 06 an: 1978
Profession: étudiante	
Adresse:	**Nationalité:** américaine
Rue: Main Street	
Numéro: 27	
Ville: Akron **Province/État:** Ohio **Code Postal:** 44313	
Pays: États-Unis	
Téléphone: 1-330-982-2018	

Adresse en France:
10 rue Servan, 69000 Lyon

Signé(e) *Jennifer Jameson*

Student Identification

Jennifer is on a plane going to Lyon, France.
Compare her passport to her landing card.

Activity A

Match the French word with its English equivalent.

1	adresse	**a**	date of birth
2	nom	**b**	last name
3	rue	**c**	address
4	date de naissance	**d**	street

Activity B

Jennifer will be studying French at a school in Lyon. Use the information above to complete the address section of her application.

CULTURE TIP

Locations in France are divided into three levels: *communes*, *départements* and *régions*. *Communes* are the smallest level. They make up the towns and cities of France, ranging from Paris or Marseille to rural villages. *Départements* are larger than *communes*. Each *département* is labeled with a number. Today there are 96 *départements* within the French borders and four overseas. *Régions* are the largest level (26 in all, including overseas). They predate the Revolution and vary widely in terms of character, tradition and cuisine.

DOSSIER DE DEMANDE D'ADMISSION

UNIVERSITÉ de Lyon

Adresse en France:

Numéro: _____

Rue: _____

Pays: _____

Ville: _____

LESSON 6

Words to Know

Core Words

Les numéros (Numbers)

zéro	0	onze	11
un	1	douze	12
deux	2	treize	13
trois	3	quatorze	14
quatre	4	quinze	15
cinq	5	seize	16
six	6	dix-sept	17
sept	7	dix-huit	18
huit	8	dix-neuf	19
neuf	9	vingt	20
dix	10	trente	30

Informations personnelles (Personal Information)

l'adresse	address
l'avenue	avenue
le numéro	number
le téléphone	telephone

Activity A

Identify the pattern in the words *dix-sept, dix-huit* and *vingt-et-un, vingt-deux, vingt-trois*. Then write the French words to complete the number sequences.

seize, dix-sept, dix-huit, _____, vingt,

vingt-et-un, vingt-deux, vingt-trois, _____, _____,

_____, _____, _____, _____, trente

SMART TIP

Watch out for these common abbreviations in French:

avenue	Av
numéro	Nº
téléphone	Tél

Conseil
Nº 29
Av Matisse
Tél 914 617 585

Activity B

Read the numbers 1–30 aloud in French. Then match each number with the correct word.

1	dix		4	douze
6	un		9	quinze
13	trente		12	quatorze
18	six		15	quatre
10	treize		22	vingt-deux
30	dix-huit		14	neuf

Activity C

Translate the following information from French to English. Use numbers instead of words when possible.

1   Rue quatorze

   _____

2   Av Victor Hugo, Nº vingt-six

   _____

3   Tél: un-sept-huit trois-sept-cinq quatre-deux-un-neuf

   _____

4   Code Postal: trois-huit-zéro-zéro-un

   _____

CULTURE TIP

In France, more people use *SMS* (text messaging) than make calls on their cell or mobile phones because it's cheaper and faster. However, French text-messaging shorthand can be very confusing to the beginner. Can you guess what *bjr sava* means? Answer: *Bonjour, ça va ?* or "Hello, how are you?"

Smart Phrases

Core Phrases

Ma date de naissance est _____.	My birthday is____.
Mon adresse est _____.	My address is____.
Mon numéro de téléphone est le ___.	My phone number is____.
Quelle est votre adresse ?	What's your address?
Quel est votre numéro de téléphone ?	What's your phone number?
Quelle est votre date de naissance ?	When's your birthday?
Où habitez-vous ?	Where do you live?

SMART TIP

When addressing a letter or an envelope in French, be sure to use the recipient's appropriate title. For a man, write *Monsieur* (abbreviated as M.). For an unmarried woman write *Mademoiselle* (Mlle), and for a married or divorced woman write *Madame* (Mme).

Activity A

Write your *nom, prénom, adresse, date de naissance* and *numéro de téléphone* in French.

nom _____
prénom _____
adresse _____
_____
date de naissance _____
numéro de téléphone _____

Activity B

Caroline is asking Daniel some questions. What is she asking?

1

Où habitez-vous ?

a the place where he lives
b the specific street where he lives

2

Quelle est votre adresse ?

a the place where he lives
b his address

3

Quel est votre numéro de téléphone ?

a his phone number
b his date of birth

4

Quelle est votre date de naissance ?

a his phone number
b his date of birth

Smart Grammar

Regular Verbs in the Present Tense

Regular verbs in French end in *–er, –ir* or *–re* in the infinitive. Look at the chart to see how to conjugate verbs in the present tense with *–er* and *–ir*. You will learn verbs with *–re* in the next unit.

Verbs with *–er*

Drop the *–er* and add the appropriate ending for each pronoun, such as with *parler* (to speak).

je	parl**e**	I speak
tu	parl**es**	you speak
il/elle	parl**e**	he/she speaks
nous	parl**ons**	we speak
vous	parl**ez**	you speak
ils/elles	parl**ent**	they speak

Examples

| Je parle. | I speak. |
| Nous parlons. | We speak. |

Activity A

Conjugate the verb *parler* in the present tense.

je _____

tu _____

il/elle _____

nous _____

vous _____

ils/elles _____

SMART TIP

When you name a series of things you can use the conjunction *et* (and): *Je parle français, anglais et espagnol* (I speak French, English and Spanish).

Verbs with *–ir*

Drop the *–ir* and add the appropriate ending for each pronoun, such as with *finir* (to finish).

je	fin**is**	I finish
tu	fin**is**	you finish
il/elle	fin**it**	he/she finishes
nous	fin**issons**	we finish
vous	fin**issez**	you finish
ils/elles	fin**issent**	they finish

Examples

| Tu finis. | You finish. |
| Vous finissez. | You finish. |

Activity B

Conjugate the verb *finir* in the present tense.

je _____

tu _____

il/elle _____

nous _____

vous _____

ils/elles _____

Activity C

Look at the pictures. Write where each person lives. Be sure to use the appropriate conjugation of *habiter*.

Nick, 10 Orchard Street

_____

Julia and Max, 24 7th Street

_____

Amy and I, 16 Main Street

_____

Your Turn

Think about the verb *enseigner* (to teach). How would you say in French that you teach English and French? How would you say that Amandine teaches English?

Activity A

How many of each do you see? Use the correct plural form when necessary.

1  _____

2  _____

3  _____

4  _____

Activity B

Use the address book to answer the following questions in French. Remember that the order of some words may change. Be sure to spell out numbers.

Thierry Gomard 25 Rue de Rivoli	05 06 45 56 66
David Bonner 15 Rue Perronet	01 61 45 17 27
Christine Brel 8 Rue Lafayette	04 33 52 75 19
Corrine & Mark Smith 30 Avenue Baudin	05 49 67 14 32

1   Où habite Thierry ?

2   Quel est le numéro de téléphone de Thierry ?

3   Où habitent Corrine et Mark ?

4   Quel est le numéro de téléphone de Christine ?

5   Où habite David ?

Challenge

Write a short paragraph about a friend. Tell where he or she lives as well as his or her address and phone number. Then try to think of one extra piece of information you can add using a regular –er or –ir verb. For example: *Il parle français* (He speaks French).

Activity C

Look at each noun and write the correct definite article. Don't forget to think about the number and gender of each noun. Then use a phrase with *Regarde…* to show each item or items.

1   _____ oiseaux   3   _____ chat

2   _____ femmes   4   _____ maison

Activity D

You've just arrived at the Marseille Language Institute to study French. Astrid, the receptionist, needs some basic information. She doesn't understand English, so you must respond in French. Fill in the blanks in the conversation.

Astrid   Bonjour ! Comment vous appelez-vous ?

Vous   _____

Astrid   Bien. Quel est votre numéro de téléphone ?

Vous   _____

Astrid   Quelle est votre adresse ?

Vous   _____

Astrid   Et le code postal ?

Vous   _____

Astrid   Pour finir, quelle est votre date de naissance ?

Vous   _____

Astrid   Excellent ! Bienvenue à l'Institut de langues de Marseille !

Vous   _____

Internet Activity

Go to **www.berlitzbooks.com/5minute** for a list of searchable satellite maps. Type in the following address for the Cinémathèque Française: *51, rue de Bercy, 75012 Paris*. Zoom in on the map. If you wanted to visit the Cinémathèque Française, where would you stay?

Unit 3 Time and Date

In this unit you will:
- tell *le temps* (the time) and *la date* (the date).
- learn the numbers 31 and up.
- conjugate regular *–re* verbs.
- learn the irregular verb *faire* (to do).

Quelle heure est-il ?

Dialogue

François and Sandrine are watching a soccer game. Listen to them talk about the time, how much time is left in the game and the score.

Sandrine Quelle heure est-il ?

François Il est dix-huit heures.

Sandrine Il est tôt ! Combien de temps reste-t-il avant la fin du match ?

François Il reste cinquante-cinq minutes.

Sandrine Quel est le score ?

François Lyon 1, Paris 0.

Activity A

Write the correct answer in French.

1 What time is it?

_____

2 Is Sandrine surprised that it's *tôt* (early)?

_____

3 How much time is left in the game?

_____

4 Which team is winning?

_____

Activity B

Put the dialogue in order.
Number the phrases 1–4.

Il reste cinquante-cinq minutes.

#

Il est dix-huit heures.

#

Quelle heure est-il ?

#

Il est tôt ! Combien de temps reste-t-il avant la fin du match ?

#

CULTURE TIPS

- In France, like most parts of Europe, the time is often read according to the 24-hour clock. For example, 6 PM is *18h00, dix-huit heures.*

- French 7:35 PM is written *19h35.*

Smart Phrases

Core Phrases

Quelle heure est-il ?	What time is it?
Il est vingt-deux heures.	It's 10 PM.
Il est sept heures et demie.	It's 7:30 AM.
Il est six heures et quart.	It's a quarter after 6.
Il est sept heures moins le quart.	It's a quarter to 7.
Il est minuit.	It's midnight.
Il est midi.	It's noon.
Il est tard !	It's late!
Il est tôt !	It's early!

Activity A

Look at the clock and write a sentence telling what time it is. Then read the sentence aloud.

Example: Il est sept heures et quart.

1 _____

2 _____

3 _____

4 _____

Activity B

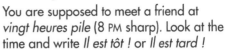

You are supposed to meet a friend at *vingt heures pile* (8 PM sharp). Look at the time and write *Il est tôt !* or *Il est tard !*

1 6h45 _____

2 20h15 _____

3 7h30 _____

4 21h00 _____

Activity C

What do you say if you want to…

1 …ask for the time?

_____

2 …say it's early?

_____

3 …say it's late?

_____

4 …say it's 2 AM?

_____

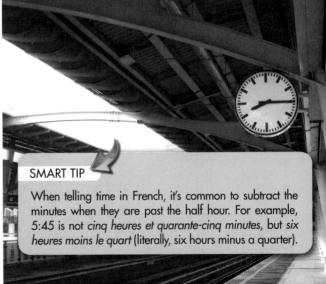

SMART TIP

When telling time in French, it's common to subtract the minutes when they are past the half hour. For example, 5:45 is not *cinq heures et quarante-cinq minutes*, but *six heures moins le quart* (literally, six hours minus a quarter).

Words to Know

Core Words

Le temps (Time)

une heure	hour
une minute	minute
une seconde	second
à _____ heures pile	at _____ o'clock sharp

Les numéros (Numbers)

trente-et-un	thirty-one
trente-deux	thirty-two
trente-trois	thirty-three
trente-quatre	thirty-four
trente-cinq	thirty-five
quarante	forty
cinquante	fifty
soixante	sixty

Extra Words

un demi/une demie	half (m/f)
un quart	quarter
matin	morning
après-midi	afternoon
soir	night

SMART TIP

Did you notice the pattern in numbers 31–35? Numbers that are between the tens (30, 40, 50, etc.) follow a pattern: 31 is thirty and one, or *trente et un*, 32 is *trente-deux,* and so on. Can you guess what 36–40 are in French?

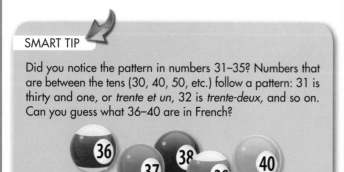

Activity A

Write the following numbers in word form.

1   44   _____

2   32   _____

3   67   _____

4   58   _____

Activity B

A show starts at *vingt heures pile* (8 PM sharp). *Combien de temps reste-t-il ?* How much time is left until the show? Write the time in word form. Be sure to use the plurals *heures* and *minutes* when the answer is more than one.

Examples:

Il reste une heure et quart.   Il reste vingt minutes.

1   _____

2   _____

3   _____

4   _____

Your Turn

It is *16h12* (4:12 PM) and you are watching a soccer game. The first half started at *16h00* (4 PM) and it lasts 45 minutes. You look at the clock every ten minutes.

Tell the time and how many minutes are left in the first half each time you look at the clock. Start at *16h12* (4:12 PM).

LESSON 4

Smart Grammar

Regular –re Verbs

To conjugate regular –re verbs such as *vendre* (to sell), drop the –re and add an ending as follows:

je	vend**s**	I sell
tu	vend**s**	you sell
il/elle	vend	he/she sells
nous	vend**ons**	we sell
vous	vend**ez**	you sell
ils/elles	vend**ent**	they sell

Examples

Il vend. He sells.
Tu vends. You sell.

Activity A

Complete the following chart to conjugate the verb *répondre* (to respond) in the present tense.

je _____

tu _____

il/elle _____

nous _____

vous _____

ils/elles _____

SMART TIP

Note that when conjugating the *il/elle* form of regular –re verbs, no extra ending is added.

Activity B

Write the correct form of each –re verb.

1 | vendre |  Je _____

2 | répondre | Nous _____

3 | descendre |  Elle _____

4 | attendre | Elles _____

Your Turn

Describe what is happening in the pictures.

attendre

descendre

escaliers

_____

_____

À faire

aller chez le médecin

faire ses devoirs

faire la lessive

appeler Romain

Things to Do

Amandine is thinking about the things she has to do today. Look at the pictures and her to-do list.

Activity A

Choose the correct answer.

1   What is the first thing Amandine has to do?
   a wash clothes   **b do homework**

2   Which phrase means "to do homework"?
   a faire ses devoirs   **b faire la lessive**

3   Which phrase means "to do"?
   a à faire   **b de faire**

4   What will Amandine do before she calls Romain?
   a faire ses devoirs   **b aller chez le boucher**

À faire
faire la lessive
aller chez le médecin
faire ses devoirs
appeler Romain

SMART TIP

The preposition *chez* (at) can be used before the name of a person or place to indicate ownership of a location, for example: *aller chez le médecin* (go to the doctor's office), *aller chez Marie* (go to Marie's house), *aller chez le boulanger* (go to the baker's).

Activity B

Write the appropriate French phrase next to each picture.

1

_____

3

_____

2

Maud
0189681833

_____

4

_____

LESSON 6

Words to Know

Core Words

Les jours de la semaine (Days of the Week)

lundi	Monday
mardi	Tuesday
mercredi	Wednesday
jeudi	Thursday
vendredi	Friday
samedi	Saturday
dimanche	Sunday

Les mois de l'année (Months of the Year)

janvier	January
février	February
mars	March
avril	April
mai	May
juin	June
juillet	July
août	August
septembre	September
octobre	October
novembre	November
décembre	December

SMART TIPS

- In French-speaking countries the date is written with the day before the month. So, November 10 would be *10/11* or *le 10 novembre*.

- All years in French are expressed as regular numbers. For example: 1999 would be *mille neuf cent quatre-vingt dix-neuf* (one thousand nine hundred ninety-nine). 2000 is *deux mille* and *2009 is deux mille neuf*.

- The names of days and months in French are not capitalized.

Activity A

Look over Romain's agenda for the week and answer the questions below.

AGENDA	
lundi	faire mes devoirs
mardi	aller chez le médecin
mercredi	faire la lessive
jeudi	faire mes devoirs
vendredi	appeler Amandine
samedi	faire la lessive
dimanche	faire la cuisine

1 What day will Romain cook? _____

2 What days will Romain do homework? _____
   et _____

3 What day will Romain call Amandine? _____

4 What day will Romain go to the doctor? _____

5 What days will Romain do laundry? _____
   et _____

Activity B

Write each date in French. Remember: The first number is the day.

Example Thursday 24/02 _____jeudi, le 24 février_____

1   Monday 17/11 _____

2   Saturday 05/06 _____

3   Wednesday 21/09 _____

4   Friday 08/04 _____

5   Tuesday 31/01 _____

6   Sunday 12/08 _____

7   Thursday 25/03 _____

8   Sunday 14/10 _____

9   Monday 29/05 _____

10 Tuesday 02/12 _____

11 Friday 15/07 _____

12 Wednesday 18/02 _____

Smart Phrases

Core Phrases

Quel jour sommes-nous ?	What day is today?
Nous sommes mardi.	Today is Tuesday.
Quelle est la date aujourd'hui ?	What's today's date?
Quel mois sommes-nous ?	What month is this?
Quelle année sommes-nous ?	What year is this?

CULTURE TIP

National holidays and vacation time are plentiful in French culture. If you are thinking of shopping in France, be sure you know which days are *jours fériés* (public holidays), because many businesses will be closed. Outside of Paris, you may also have a hard time finding places to shop on Sundays and on Monday afternoons.

Activity A

Circle the best response.

1 Quel jour sommes-nous ?

   a janvier   **b** mardi

2 Quel mois sommes-nous ?

   a lundi   **b** décembre

3 Quelle est la date aujourd'hui ?

   a C'est le 18 décembre 2010.   **b** Nous sommes mercredi.

4 Quelle année sommes-nous ?

   a le 23 août   **b** 2009

Activity B

Write the appropriate French questions to complete the mini-conversations.

1 _____ ?   Nous sommes lundi.

2 _____ ?   le 18 juin

3 _____ ?   avril

4 _____ ?   2010

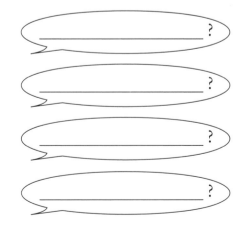
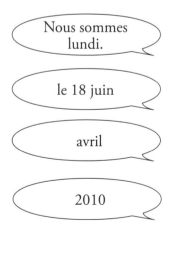

Smart Grammar

The Verb *faire* (to Do)

The verb *faire* is irregular. The chart shows its conjugation in the present tense.

je	fais	I do
tu	fais	you do
il/elle	fait	he/she does
nous	faisons	we do
vous	faites	you do
ils/elles	font	they do

Activity A

Fill in the blanks with the correct conjugation of *faire.*

1 Je _____ la lessive le dimanche.

2 Eve _____ la cuisine le samedi.

3 Christine et Lisette _____ leurs devoirs le jeudi.

4 Isabelle et moi _____ la cuisine le vendredi soir.

CULTURE TIP

In most French-speaking countries "to wash" is expressed as *laver.* For example, you *laver les mains* (wash your hands), but with laundry you *faire la lessive* (literally, do the laundry).

SMART TIP

Faire is a very common verb in French, and while it often translates as "to do," there are many instances where it has other meanings. For example the phrase *faire un gâteau* means "to make a cake." *Faire du football* means "to play soccer." And *faire des achats* means "to go shopping."

Activity B

Qu'est-ce qu'ils font ? Match each picture with a phrase to tell what each person is doing.

1 Il fait du café. _____

2 Ils font des plans. _____

3 Elle fait un gâteau. _____

4 Elles font du football. _____

Your Turn

Write sentences telling what activities you do on Saturdays and Sundays. Be sure to use the correct form of the verb *faire.*

_____

_____

Activity A

Choose activities from the box to tell what Amélie has to do. Use the *elle* form of each verb. The first one has been done for you.

> allez chez le médecin   faire ses devoirs   faire la cuisine
> faire la lessive   appeler Alain

1   Amélie va chez le médecin à neuf heures et demie.

2   _____

3   _____

4   _____

5   _____

Activity B

Look at the following times and use the example to write how much time is left in the game.

Example   1h31mn02s   Il reste une heure, trente et une minutes et deux secondes.

1   2h34mn13s   _____

2   1h10mn   _____

3   0h12mn39s   _____

4   1h27mn25s   _____

Activity C

André lost his planner and forgot his schedule for March. Look at the calendar, then answer the questions.

mars						
lundi	mardi	mercredi	jeudi	vendredi	samedi	dimanche
1	2	3 faire la lessive	4	5	6	7
8	9	10	11	12	13 faire mes devoirs	14
15 appeler Marcus	16	17	18	19	20	21 faire la cuisine
22	23 laver la voiture	24	25	26	27	28

On what dates has André scheduled the following activities? Write the date as the weekday/day/month. Write out the numbers in French.

Example do the laundry

_____ mercredi, le trois mars 2009 _____

1   cook

_____

2   do homework

_____

3   wash the car

_____

4   call Marcus

_____

Internet Activity

Imagine you are planning a trip to France. Go to **www.berlitbooks.com/5minute** for a list of sites in French where you can browse for train tickets. Use your knowledge of dates and times in French to search for non-stop trips from Lille to Paris. Which will get you in on Friday evening? On Saturday morning?

Challenge

Write a paragraph about a friend. Tell what he or she learns, studies and does.

Unit 4 Family

In this unit you will:
- introduce your immediate family and talk about your relatives.
- study possessive and demonstrative adjectives.
- use indefinite articles.
- learn the irregular verb *avoir* (to have).

LESSON 1

Photo de famille

Claire et ses parents

Patrice

Jean-Pierre et Monique

Muriel

Dialogue

Claire and Sam are talking about their families. Listen as Claire shows Sam pictures of her family and tells him who each person is.

Sam Vous êtes combien dans ta famille, Claire ?

Claire Dans ma famille, nous sommes sept. Regarde la photo.

Sam Quelle grande famille ! Ici, c'est toi, et là, ce sont tes parents, non ?

Claire Oui. Ici, c'est ma mère et là, c'est mon père. Et cette fille, c'est ma petite sœur, Muriel.

Sam Et là, ce sont tes frères ?

Claire Oui. Ici, c'est mon frère aîné, Jean-Pierre. Et là, c'est Patrice, mon frère cadet.

Sam Et là, qui est-ce ?

Claire C'est Monique, la femme de Jean-Pierre.

Activity A

Circle **T** for true or **F** for false.

1 There are fewer than five people in Claire's family. **T/F**

2 Monique is Claire's mother. **T/F**

3 Claire has three brothers. **T/F**

4 Muriel is Claire's sister. **T/F**

Activity B

Read the following phrases. Circle the picture that illustrates each phrase.

1 C'est mon père.   a   b

2 C'est ma sœur.   a   b

3 C'est ma mère.   a   b

4 Ce sont mes frères.   a   b

CULTURE TIPS

- In French, an informal way of talking about your parents is to call your mother *maman* rather than *mère*, and your father *papa* rather than *père*.

- The most common words for "husband" and "wife" are *mari* and *femme*, but you may also hear the words *époux* (m) and *épouse* (f), literally meaning "spouse." These terms are common in official documents.

LESSON 2
Words to Know

Core Words

les enfants	children
la famille	family
la femme	wife
la fille	daughter
le fils	son
le frère	brother
le mari	husband
la mère	mother
les parents	parents
le père	father
la sœur	sister

Extra Words

aîné/aînée	older (m/f)
cadet/cadette	younger (m/f)

Sam's Family Tree

Thomas   Hélène

Sam   Rachel   Paul

SMART TIP

In the word *sœur* the letters *o* and *e* are linked into a single letter œ called a "ligature." Other examples in French include the words *œuf* (egg) and *œuvre* (work of art).

SMART TIPS

There are two ways to talk about possession:

- by using possessive pronouns such as *mon/ma* (m/f) (my). You will learn these pronouns in Lesson 4.
- by using the definite article + noun (possession) + *de*. For example: *le mari de Christine* (Christine's husband).

Activity A

Look at Sam's family tree. Complete his description. The first one is done for you.

Il y a cinq personnes dans ma ___famille___. Thomas,

c'est mon _____. Ma _____
               father   mother

s'appelle Hélène. Rachel, c'est ma _____.
                                           sister

Paul est le _____ de Rachel.
                   husband

Activity B

Circle the correct word.

1   Sam et Rachel sont **frère et sœur   parents**.

2   Sam est le **frère   père** de Rachel.

3   Hélène est la **mère   père** de Sam et de Rachel.

4   Thomas est le **fils   père** de Sam et de Rachel.

5   Hélène et Thomas sont les **sœur et frère   parents** de Sam et de Rachel.

6   Sam est le **mari   fils** d'Hélène et de Thomas.

7   Rachel est la **fille   fils** d'Hélène et de Thomas.

8   Sam et Rachel sont les **parents   enfants** d'Hélène et de Thomas.

9   Rachel est la **mari   femme** de Paul.

10 Paul est le **mari   frère** de Rachel.

Smart Phrases

Core Phrases

Vous êtes combien dans votre famille ?

Dans ma famille, nous sommes _____.

Ma famille est grande/petite.

Quelle jolie famille !

Quelle grande/petite famille !

How big is your family?

There are _____ of us in the family.

My family is big/small.

What a nice family!

What a big/small family!

Activity A

Put the phrases in order to create a dialogue.

Vous êtes combien dans ta famille ?

#1

Oui, ma famille est grande. Est-ce que ta famille est grande ?

#

Dans ma famille, nous sommes huit. Regarde la photo.

#

Quelle grande famille !

#

Non. Ma famille est petite. Dans ma famille, nous sommes quatre.

#

Activity B

Write a phrase to tell whether each family is big or small.

1 _____

2 _____

3 _____

4 _____

Your Turn

Use your new vocabulary and phrases to talk about your family. Is it big or small? Do you have any siblings? How many?

Smart Grammar

Possessive Adjectives

Possessive adjectives agree in number and gender with the noun to which they refer. *Notre/nos* (our), *votre/vos* (your) and *leur/leurs* (their) agree in number only with the noun to which they refer.

Singular	Plural	English
mon/ma	mes	my (m/f)
ton/ta	tes	your (m/f, inf.)
son/sa	ses	his/her/its (m/f)
notre	nos	our
votre	vos	your (form.)
leur	leurs	their

Examples

C'est mon frère. — He's my brother.
Ce sont tes sœurs. — They're your sisters.
Sa famille est grande. — His/Her family is big.
Notre mère s'appelle Karen. — Our mother's name is Karen.

Activity A

Fill in the blanks with the correct possessive adjectives. They may be either singular or plural, masculine or feminine, depending on the object.

1 C'est _____ mère. (my)

2 Est-ce que c'est _____ frère ? (your, inf.)

3 _____ famille est petite. (your, form.)

4 Ce sont _____ sœurs. (my)

5 Ce sont _____ parents ? (your, inf.)

6 Ces hommes sont _____ frères. (your, form.)

7 _____ maison est grande. (our)

8 Les enfants sont _____ fils. (our)

Demonstrative Adjectives

A demonstrative adjective agrees in gender and number with the noun to which it refers. When talking about mixed gender groups, use the masculine plural demonstrative adjective.

Singular	English	Plural	English
ce	this/that (m)	ces	these/those (m/f)
cet	this/that (m) (before a vowel)		
cette	this/that (f)		

Activity B

Read the sentences below. Write the letter of the corresponding picture next to each sentence.

1 Ces filles sont mes filles. _____

2 Cette voiture est ma voiture. _____

3 Cet homme est mon père. _____

4 Cette maison est ma maison. _____

5 Cette femme, c'est ma mère. _____

6 Ce couple, ce sont mes parents. _____

7 Ces chiens sont mes chiens. _____

8 Ces garcons sont mes frères. _____

SMART PRONUNCIATION

Use the demonstrative adjective *cet* rather than *ce* in front of a masculine noun that begins with *h*. If the noun is feminine—*horloge* (clock), for example—use the feminine demonstrative adjective: *cette horloge*.

Nadine
(grand-mère)

Joseph
(grand-père)

Family Tree

Pauline Dauphin just created a family tree for her records. Look at the tree and read each relationship aloud.

Karen
(tante)

André
(oncle)

Muriel
(mère)

Pierre
(père)

Activity A

Describe the relationship in French of each person to Pauline.

1 André est _____

2 Muriel est _____

3 Georges est _____

4 Karen est _____

Robert
(cousin)

Anita
(cousine)

Pauline

Georges
(frère)

Sandrine
(belle-sœur)

Jérôme
(neveu)

Annie
(nièce)

Activity B

Can you tell who's who in Pauline's family? Write the relationship of each person under his or her picture.

CULTURE TIP

Add the prefix *beau-* or *belle-* (m/f) to the names of family members for your step-family, just like your in-laws: *beau-père, belle-mère, beau-fils* and *belle-fille*. But for "stepbrother" and "stepsister," you say *demi-frère* and *demi-sœur* (literally half-brother and half-sister).

1

_____

2

_____

3

_____

4

_____

LESSON 6

Words to Know

Core Words

la grand-mère	grandmother
le grand-père	grandfather
les grands-parents	grandparents
la tante	aunt
l'oncle	uncle
le cousin	cousin (m)
la cousine	cousin (f)
le petit-fils	grandson
la petite-fille	granddaughter
le neveu	nephew
la nièce	niece

Extra Words

le beau-père	father-in-law
la belle-mère	mother-in-law
le beau-frère	brother-in-law
la belle-sœur	sister-in-law
le beau-fils	son-in-law
la belle-fille	daughter-in-law

Activity A

> petit-fils   cousine   neveu
>
> grand-parents   grand-père   tante

Match the French word with its English equivalent.

1 cousin (f) _____

2 nephew _____

3 aunt _____

4 grandson _____

5 grandfather _____

6 grandparents _____

Activity B

How are you related? Complete the statements by circling the correct relative.

1 La sœur de ma mère est ma _____
   a tante   **b cousine**

2 Le fils de ma tante est mon _____
   a cousin   **b cousine**

3 La mère de mon père est ma _____
   a grand-mère   **b grand-père**

4 Le cousin de mon fils est mon _____
   a neveu   **b nièce**

5 Le père de mon père est mon _____
   a grand-père   **b oncle**

6 La nièce de mon père est ma _____
   a cousin   **b cousine**

> **SMART TIP**
>
> Many names for family members in French, such as *grand-mère* and *oncle*, look like and have a similar meaning to the equivalent English words. These are called cognates. Cognates are common between English and French and are often a useful aid in decoding unfamiliar words. But watch out for false cognates such as the French verb *blesser*, which resembles the English verb "to bless" but actually means "to wound, injure or offend."

Smart Phrases

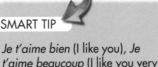

SMART TIP

Je t'aime bien (I like you), *Je t'aime beaucoup* (I like you very much) and *Je t'adore* (I adore you) can be used to express love to family members and friends.
Je t'aime (I love you) is reserved for a romantic partner.

Je t'aime.

Core Phrases

Avez-vous de la famille à _____ ?	Do you have any relatives in _____?
Votre famille est-elle proche ?	Is your family close?
J'ai une famille proche.	My family is close.
Êtes-vous marié/mariée ?	Are you married? (m/f)
Je suis célibataire.	I'm single.
J'aime ma famille.	I love my family.
Je t'aime.	I love you.

Activity A

Draw a line to match the questions and statements with the correct response.

1 Avez-vous de la famille à Paris?

2 Ton frère est très mignon ! Est-il célibataire ?

3 Aimez-vous vos beaux-parents ?

4 Êtes-vous célibataire ?

(a) Non, ma femme est là.

(b) Oui, j'aime beaucoup mes beaux-parents.

(c) Non, il est marié.

(d) Non, je n'ai pas de la famille en France.

Activity B

What do you say if you want to...

1 ...tell your husband/wife that you love him/her?

_____

2 ...tell your mother that you love her?

_____

3 ...tell someone that your family is close?

_____

4 ...ask someone if he/she is married?

_____

Your Turn

Now talk about you and your relatives. Are you single or married? Who is married in your family? Who is single?

LESSON 8

Smart Grammar

Indefinite Articles

French has three indefinite articles. Each article agrees with its noun in number and gender.

un	a/an	(m, sing.)
une	a/an	(f, sing.)
des	some	(m/f, pl.)

Activity A

Write the noun and the correct indefinite article next to each picture.

1 _____

2 _____

3 _____

4 _____

The Verb *avoir* (to Have)

The verb *avoir* is irregular. Look at the chart for its conjugation in the present tense.

j'	ai	I have
tu	as	you have
il/elle	a	he/she has
nous	avons	we have
vous	avez	you have
ils/elles	ont	they have

Examples

| Il a une cousine. | He has a cousin. |
| Nous avons un oncle. | We have an uncle. |

Activity B

Write a sentence using the correct form of *avoir*.

1 tu, frère   _____

2 je, cousin   _____

3 elles, tantes   _____

4 vous, nièces   _____

Your Turn

Answer the following questions about your family.

1 Avez-vous des tantes ?   _____

2 Avez-vous des neveux ?   _____

3 Vos oncles ont-ils des enfants ?   _____

4 Vos cousins ont-ils des enfants ?   _____

SMART TIP

The verb *avoir* is sometimes used as the equivalent of the verb "to be," in the English sense. If you want to say "I'm hungry," you would say *J'ai faim*, which literally means "I have hunger." "I'm thirsty" is *J'ai soif*, and "I'm cold" is *J'ai froid*.

Activity A

Monique has brought her new boyfriend Antoine to a family party and is pointing out family members to him. Fill in the blanks of Monique and Antoine's conversation.

Monique Voici mon _____, Alain. Et voilà
          grandfather
ma _____, Nathalie.
   grandmother

Antoine Et qui est cette femme ?

Monique C'est ma _____, Michelle, et c'est
                cousin
son _____, Didier.
      brother

Antoine Cette dame, c'est ta _____ ?
                              mother

Monique Non, c'est ma _____, Carmen.
                      aunt
C'est la _____ de ma mère.
            sister
Michelle et Didier sont ses _____.
                              children

Antoine Alors, ta mère, c'est cette dame ?

Monique (laughs) Non, c'est ma _____
                              aunt
Lisette, la _____ de mon
            the wife
_____ Maurice. C'est le _____
   uncle   brother
de mon _____.
         father

Antoine Ta _____ est grande. Mais où est
              family
(where is) ta mère ?

Monique Mes _____ ne sont pas ici (are not here).
                parents

Activity B

Tell how each person is related to Monique. Use the correct form of the possessive adjectives *son/sa/ses* before the person's title.

Example Alain est son grand-père.

1   Nathalie _____

2   Michelle et Didier _____

3   Carmen et Lisette _____

4   Maurice _____

Activity C

At the party, Maurice asks Antoine questions about his family. Fill in Antoine's responses to Maurice's questions.

Maurice Ta famille est-t-elle grande ou petite ?

Antoine _____

Maurice As-tu des frères ?

Antoine _____

Maurice As-tu des oncles ?

Antoine _____

Activity D

Now Antoine is talking to *grand-père* Alain. Fill in the blanks with the correct demonstrative adjective.

Antoine _____ homme, c'est votre neveu ?
              This/That

Alain Non, c'est le neveu de monsieur.

Antoine Qui est _____ femme ?
                      this/that

Alain _____ femme, c'est ma nièce.
            This/That

Antoine _____ filles sont vos filles ?
              These/Those

Alain Non, _____ filles sont mes petite-filles.
                these/those

Activity E

Write a sentence telling how many children each parent has.

1

_____

2

_____

3

_____

4

_____

Internet Activity

Go to **www.berlitzbooks.com/5minute** for a list of sites in French where you can create a family tree. Create a family tree and label all your relatives in French. Practice introducing your relatives aloud.

Unit 5   Meals

In this unit you will:
- discuss breakfast, lunch and dinner.
- use food and drink vocabulary.
- form questions in French.
- use the irregular verb *vouloir* (to want).

J'ai faim !

Dialogue

Isabelle and Rémy talk about what they want to eat. Listen as they discuss food for *le petit-déjeuner* (breakfast), *le déjeuner* (lunch) and *le dîner* (dinner).

Isabelle J'ai faim. Est-ce que tu veux prendre ton petit-déjeuner ?

Rémy Oui. J'ai envie d'une salade.

Isabelle À huit heures du matin ? On mange de la salade au déjeuner ou au dîner.

Rémy Ça m'est égal. Qu'est-ce que tu veux ?

Isabelle Des œufs. Veux-tu manger des œufs ?

Rémy Oui. Et j'ai aussi envie de boire du vin.

Isabelle On ne boit pas de vin au petit-déjeuner !

Activity A

Circle **T** for true and **F** for false.

1 Isabelle wants to eat breakfast.   **T/F**
2 Rémy wants to eat salad for breakfast.   **T/F**
3 Isabelle tells Rémy that they should have soup.   **T/F**
4 Rémy is in the mood for a beer.   **T/F**

Activity B

Circle the correct answer.

1 What does Isabelle want to eat?
   a   b

2 What is Rémy in the mood to drink?
   a   b

3 What are they going to eat for breakfast?
   a    b

4 What time does the dialogue take place?
   a   b

> **SMART TIP**
>
> The preposition *de* has several meanings and uses, including:
> - of (belonging)
> - of (made of)
> - quantity (*beaucoup de*)
> - from
> - as a link for certain verbs (*j'ai envie de prendre un petit-déjeuner*)
>
> When speaking about what you eat or drink, use *de* with the appropriate definite article. Note that with *le* and *les* you use a contraction.
>
> - de + le = du
> - de + la = de la
> - de + l' = de l'
> - de + les = des

LESSON 2
Words to Know

Core Words

La nourriture (Food)

les fruits	fruit (m)
les œufs	eggs (m)
le pain	bread
la salade	salad
la soupe	soup

Les boissons (Drinks)

la bière	beer
le café	coffee
l'eau	water (f)
le jus	juice
le lait	milk
le thé	tea

Food Verbs

boire	to drink
manger	to eat
prendre	to take/eat/drink

CULTURE TIP

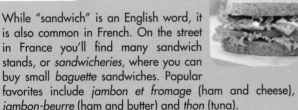

While "sandwich" is an English word, it is also common in French. On the street in France you'll find many sandwich stands, or *sandwicheries*, where you can buy small *baguette* sandwiches. Popular favorites include *jambon et fromage* (ham and cheese), *jambon-beurre* (ham and butter) and *thon* (tuna).

Activity A

Look at the pictures and write, in French, the food or drink that each person enjoys.

1 _____   2 _____

3 _____   4 _____

Activity B

Use the word bank below to tell what you eat and drink for breakfast, lunch and dinner. Be sure to use the conjunction *et* (and).

des fruits	du pain	de la bière
de la soupe	de l'eau	du café

1 le petit-déjeuner _____

2 le déjeuner _____

3 le dîner _____

SMART TIP

Think of *prendre* as the French equivalent of "to have" in regards to food and drink. If you want to say that you can't have coffee, say *Je ne peux pas prendre de café.*

LESSON 3

Smart Phrases

Core Phrases

Déjeunons.	Let's have lunch.
Dînons.	Let's have dinner.
J'ai envie de boire ___.	I'm in the mood to drink ___.
J'ai envie de manger ___.	I'm in the mood to eat ___.
J'ai faim.	I'm hungry.
Je prends ___.	I'll have ___.
J'ai soif.	I'm thirsty.
Je voudrais ___.	I would like ___.
Prenons le petit-déjeuner.	Let's have breakfast.

SMART TIP

The nouns *déjeuner* (lunch) and *dîner* (dinner) can be made into verbs: *Je vais dîner avec Marc* (I'm going to have dinner with Marc), *Nous allons déjeuner ensemble* (We will have lunch together) or simply *Déjeunons* (Let's have lunch).

Activity A

Four people want different things to eat or drink. Read the items on the left and decide if the person is hungry or thirsty. Check the appropriate answer.

		J'ai faim.	**J'ai soif.**
1	du pain et des fruits	☐	☐
2	de l'eau et du café	☐	☐
3	de la soupe et de la salade	☐	☐
4	de la bière et du vin	☐	☐

Activity B

Fill in the blanks with the correct French phrase.

1 _____ une salade.
   I'm in the mood to eat

2 _____ une bière.
   I'm in the mood to drink

Activity C

Write the correct French phrase.

1   Let's have breakfast.

2   Let's have lunch.

3   Let's have dinner.

LESSON 4

Smart Grammar

Question Words

Comment ?	How?
Lequel/Laquelle ?	Which one? (m/f, sing.)
Lesquels/Lesquelles ?	Which ones? (m/f, pl.)
Où ?	Where?
Pourquoi ?	Why?
Quand ?	When?
Quel/Quelle ?	What/Which? (m/f, sing.)
Quels/Quelles ?	What/Which? (m/f, pl.)
Qui est ?	Who is?
Qui sont ?	Who are?
Quoi ?	What?

Activity A
Fill in the blanks with the correct question word. Choose the word from the word box.

qui	où	quel/quelle
quoi	quand	

1 _____ est-ce que vous habitez ?

2 _____ est votre adresse ?

3 _____ est cette fille ?

4 _____ est-ce que vous allez au cinéma ?

5 _____ sont vos amis ?

6 _____ heure est-il ?

7 De _____ est-ce que vous avez envie de boire ?

8 _____ de ces filles est votre sœur ?

Activity B
Ask questions using the following question words.

1 Quelle _____ ?

2 Quand _____ ?

3 Qui est _____ ?

4 Où _____ ?

Activity C
What question word do you use to ask…

1 …for a reason? _____

2 …who someone is? _____

3 …when an event is going to happen? _____

4 …which object someone is pointing to? _____

5 …where someone lives? _____

Your Turn
Read the following answers. Then ask a question for each answer. Practice this in front of a mirror.

1 Ma mère s'appelle Marie.

2 Il est trois heures de l'après-midi.

3 Ce sont les cousins d'Henri.

4 J'habite à Paris.

SMART TIPS

- To begin an open-ended question, start with a question word and then use a conjugated verb. Note that *est-ce que* should be added after the question word, except with *qui*, *quel* and *lequel*.

Examples:

Qui est votre ami ?	Who is your friend?
Quand est-ce que nous mangeons ?	When do we eat?
Pourquoi est-ce que vous travaillez chaque jour ?	Why do you work every day?

- *Quel/Quelle* and *quoi* both mean "what" in French, but they are used for different grammatical functions. *Quel/Quelle* comes before the noun, agrees in gender and number and acts as the English "which": *Quel livre est-ce que tu aimes le plus ?* (Which book do you like the most?). *Quoi* is an informal form of "what" and usually comes after the verb: *C'est quoi, ça ?* (What's that?)

Dans un restaurant

Menu

Read the menu aloud. Next, listen to the dialogue. Anaïs talks to *le serveur* (the waiter) about what she will order at the restaurant.

Restaurant Madeleine

Menu

Entrées
Salade
Quiche lorraine

Plats principaux
Poisson aux légumes
Poulet aux pommes de terre
Steak frites

Desserts
Tarte au chocolat
Glace

Dialogue

Serveur Bonjour. Voulez-vous une entrée ?

Anaïs Oui. Comme entrée, je voudrais une salade.

Serveur Très bien. Et comme plat principal ?

Anaïs Que me conseillez-vous ?

Serveur Le poisson aux légumes est délicieux.

Anaïs Je ne veux pas de poisson. Je n'aime pas ça.

Serveur Le steak frites est très bien aussi.

Anaïs D'accord. Je prends le steak frites.

Serveur Très bien. Je vous sers tout de suite.

Activity A

Circle the correct picture based on the dialogue and the menu.

1 What does Anaïs want for her appetizer?

2 What does Anaïs want for her main course?

3 What else can Anaïs have for the main course that she does not choose?

4 What is an option for dessert on the menu?

Activity B

Number the phrases 1–4 to create a dialogue.

____ Comme entrée, je prends une salade.

____ Et comme plat principal ?

____ Quelle entrée voulez-vous ?

____ Je voudrais le poulet aux pommes de terre.

Words to Know

Core Words

le fromage	cheese
le gâteau	cake
la glace	ice cream
les légumes	vegetables (m)
les pâtes	pasta (f)
le poisson	fish
les pommes de terre	potatoes (f)
le poulet	chicken
le riz	rice
la tarte	pie
la viande	meat

Activity A

Decide whether each set of food items is an appetizer, a main course or a dessert. On the lines provided, write *entrée, plat principal* or *dessert.*

1 la salade et la quiche lorraine _____

2 la viande et le poisson _____

3 la glace et la tarte au chocolat _____

4 le poulet et les pâtes _____

Activity B

Use the menu to answer the following questions in French.

1 Quelle est l'entrée ?

2 Quel est le plat principal ?

3 Quel est le dessert ?

Your Turn

Use your new vocabulary and phrases to create your own menu.

Restaurant _____

Menu

Entrées

_____

_____

Plats principaux

_____

_____

Desserts

_____

_____

Boissons

_____

_____

Smart Phrases

Core Phrases

Bon appétit.	Enjoy your meal.
C'est bon ?	Is it good?
C'est délicieux !	This is delicious!
C'est moi qui offre.	It's on me.
L'addition, s'il vous plaît.	The check, please.
Le plat du jour est _____.	The special is _____.
Puis-je voir la carte des vins, s'il vous plaît ?	May I see the wine list?
Quel est le plat du jour ?	What's today's special?

Activity A

What do you say if you want to…

1   …tell someone to enjoy his/her meal?

_____

2   …ask the waiter for the check?

_____

3   …say that something tastes delicious?

_____

4   …ask for the wine list?

_____

CULTURE TIP

A typical French *petit-déjeuner* can include croissants, cereal or bread and coffee or hot chocolate. *Le déjeuner* is often the main meal of the day, consisting of four courses, starting around 1PM and lasting two to three hours in more formal situations. *Le dîner* is usually around 8 or 9PM and is lighter than *le déjeuner*, though for many it is becoming the main meal of the day.

Activity B

Circle the best response to the questions and scenarios below.

1   Quel est le plat du jour ?

   a   C'est délicieux !

   b   Le plat du jour est un poisson aux légumes.

2   It is the beginning of the meal and you want something to drink. You say to *le serveur*:

   a   Puis-je voir la carte des vins ?

   b   Bon appétit !

3   You are eating and the waiter asks: *C'est bon ?* You answer:

   a   Bon appétit.

   b   C'est délicieux !

4   It is the end of the meal. You say to *le serveur*:

   a   L'addition, s'il vous plaît.

   b   Quel est le plat du jour ?

Your Turn

You are at a restaurant with a friend. Tell him about the food, the menu and the specials. Ask him about his food. At the end, be polite and take care of the check.

Smart Grammar

The verb *vouloir* (to want)

The verb *vouloir* is irregular. The chart shows its conjugation in the present tense.

je	veux	I want
tu	veux	you want
il/elle	veut	he/she wants
nous	voulons	we want
vous	voulez	you want
ils/elles	veulent	they want

SMART TIPS

- To order at a restaurant, it is common to say *je voudrais* (the conditional form) rather than *je veux*. When making requests it is more polite to use this form: *je voudrais, tu voudrais, il/elle voudrait, nous voudrions, vous voudriez, ils/elles voudraient.*

- If you don't want something, simply put *ne* before *vouloir* and *pas* after: *Je ne veux pas de viande* (I don't want meat).

- When saying what you like or prefer, use the verb *aimer bien* (to like): *J'aime bien la salade* (I like/prefer salad).

Activity A

Write the correct present tense form of the verb *vouloir* to complete the sentences.

1   Elle ne _____ pas le poulet pour le plat principal.

2   Nous _____ le poisson.

3   Ils _____ la tarte au chocolat pour le dessert.

4   _____-vous la viande pour le plat principal ?

Activity B

What do you want to eat? Complete the sentences below with the *je* form of *vouloir* to explain what you do and don't want to eat.

1   _____ _____ pour l'entrée.
      I want   chicken

2   _____ _____ pour l'entrée.
      I don't want   cheese

3   _____ _____ pour le plat principal.
      I want   fish

4   _____ _____ pour le plat principal.
      I don't want   meat

5   _____ _____ pour le dessert.
      I want   cake

6   _____ _____ pour le dessert.
      I don't want   ice cream

Your Turn

Voulez-vous de la viande ou des légumes ? Say out loud which food items you want to eat. Then use *aimer bien* to say that you like these food items. Look at the Smart Tip or refer to the answer key for help with *aimer bien*.

le poisson

la salade

le poulet

les pommes de terre

Activity A

Look at the pictures, then write complete sentences to say what people want for lunch and what they like for dinner. Use the personal pronouns *je, tu, il/elle, nous, vous* and *ils/elles*. For each section, one sentence has been done for you.

Le déjeuner (vouloir)

1 Je veux de la soupe et boire de l'eau.
2 _____
3 _____
4 _____
5 _____
6 _____

Le dîner (aimer bien)

1 _____
2 _____
3 _____
4 _____
5 _____
6 Ils aiment bien du steak et boire de la bière.

Activity B

There has been a mix-up with the menus at Café Français. Someone put desserts under appetizers and main dishes under desserts! Cross out the mistakes and replace them with the correct words.

> **CAFÉ FRANÇAIS**
>
> **Menu**
>
> **Entrées**
> Tarte au chocolat
> Salade
>
> **Plats principaux**
> Poulet aux légumes
> Quiche lorraine
>
> **Desserts**
> Steak frites

Activity C

Julien is hungry, so Eve and he go out to dinner. Use the phrases and question words you learned in this unit to fill in the blanks of their dialogue.

Julien _____ faim.

Eve Qu'est-ce que tu _____ manger ?

Julien _____ de manger du poulet.

Eve Allons au _____.

In the car

Julien _____ est le restaurant ?

Eve C'est par là. (Points to a restaurant down the block.)

At the restaurant before eating

Eve Qu'est-ce que tu _____ pour le plat principal ?

Julien Je voudrais _____.

At the restaurant after eating

Eve _____, s'il vous plaît.

Challenge

Look at the word *banane*. What do you think it means? After you take a guess at its meaning, look up the word in a French-English dictionary to see if you're right. Then look up other kinds of fruit to expand your vocabulary. You can repeat the activity with other food items as well. Visit **www.berlitzbooks.com/5minute** for a list of online dictionaries.

Internet Activity

Many restaurants have French-language menus. Go to **www.berlitzbooks.com/5minute** for a list of sites in French to browse. Look for a menu from a restaurant in France or Canada. Read the menu out loud. *Quelles sont les entrées* ? *Les plats principaux* ? *Les desserts* ? If you don't know what certain words mean, write them down and look them up.

Unit 6 Weather and Temperature

In this unit, you will:

- talk about temperature, weather and seasons.
- learn about reflexive verbs.
- learn about qualitative adjectives.
- describe daily activities.

LESSON 1

Quel temps fait-il ?

Dialogue

Olivier lives in Fort-de-France, Martinique, and Noémie lives in Paris, France. Listen to their phone conversation about the weather in their countries.

Olivier Bonjour, Noémie. Quel temps fait-il à Paris ?

Noémie Il fait froid. Il y a du soleil mais il fait zéro degré Celsius.

Olivier Ah bon ? À Fort-de-France aussi il fait mauvais.

Noémie Quelle température fait-il ?

Olivier Trente-cinq degrés Celsius et il pleut beaucoup.

Noémie Trente-cinq degrés Celsius ? Il fait chaud !

Activity B

Read the dialogue again and look for cognates (French words that look similar to their English equivalents), then complete the crossword puzzle based on the cognate clues below.

ACROSS
2 temperature
DOWN
1 Celsius
3 degrees

SMART TIP

If you want to say "also" or "too" in French, use *aussi*.
For example:
En Suisse aussi, il fait froid.   It's also cold in Switzerland.
Moi aussi, j'ai froid.   I'm cold too.

Activity A

Match the questions with the correct picture.

1 Quel temps fait-il à Paris ? _____

2 Quel temps fait-il à Fort-de-France ? _____

3 Quelle température fait-il à Paris ? _____

4 Quelle température fait-il à Fort-de-France ? _____

ⓐ  ⓑ  ⓒ  ⓓ

Words to Know

Core Words

bon	warm
chaud	hot
froid	cold
humide	humid
la neige	snow
le nuage	cloud
la pluie	rain
le soleil	sun
le temps	weather
le vent	wind

Activity A

Use the vocabulary to complete the dialogue.

Quel _____ fait-il à Haïti ?
weather

Il fait _____ et il y a du _____.
hot   sun

Quelle _____ fait-il ?
temperature

Environ trente-cinq _____.
degrees Celsius

Ah bon ? Ici il fait _____.
Il fait moins dix.   cold

Activity B

Circle the appropriate word or phrase to complete each thought.

1   It's a nice day.

    a Il fait 25 degrés Celsius.   **b Il fait froid.**

2   It's 2 degrees Celsius.

    a Il fait froid.   **b Il fait chaud.**

3   It's raining and it's windy. This describes:

    a la température   **b le temps**

4   It's 6 degrees Celsius outside. This is:

    a le temps   **b la température**

Activity C

Match the appropriate word to each picture.

1   les nuages   **a**

2   le soleil   **b**

3   le vent   **c**

4   la pluie   **d**

5   la neige   **e**

Smart Phrases

Core Phrases

Il fait ___ degrés Celsius.	It's ___ degrees Celsius.
Il fait chaud/froid.	It's hot/cold.
Il y a du soleil.	It's sunny.
Il fait mauvais/beau.	The weather is bad/nice.
Quelle température fait-il ?	What's the temperature?
Quel temps fait-il ?	What's the weather like?

Extra Phrases

Il y a des nuages.	It's cloudy.
Il y a du soleil.	It's sunny.
Il y a du vent.	It's windy.
Il pleut.	It's raining.
Il neige.	It's snowing.

CULTURE TIP

If someone is talking about the weather and you hear *Il pleut des cordes*, you better bring an umbrella. Literally meaning "It's raining ropes," it is equivalent to the English phrase "It's raining cats and dogs."

Activity A

Write each word or phrase in the appropriate column.

35°C	Il fait chaud.	6°C
Il fait mauvais.	32°F	Il fait froid.

Quelle température fait-il ?   Quel temps fait-il ?

_____   _____

_____   _____

_____   _____

Activity B

Quel temps fait-il ? Match each picture with the best description of the weather.

1    **a** Il fait chaud.

2    **b** Il y a du soleil.

3    **c** Il fait mauvais.

4    **d** Il fait froid.

Activity C

Imagine it is a warm spring day. Read the questions and circle the appropriate responses.

1 Quel temps fait-il ?

   a Il fait beau.   **b Il fait mauvais.**

2 Fait-il chaud ou froid ?

   a Il fait chaud.   **b Il fait froid.**

3 Quelle température fait-il ?

   a Il fait cinq degrés Celsius.   **b Il fait vingt degrés Celsius.**

LESSON 4

Smart Grammar

SMART TIP

Another adjective that changes place depending on its meaning is *ancien/ancienne*. When placed before the noun it means "former" or "no longer." For example: *Il est ancien professeur* means "He is a former teacher." When placed after the noun it means "old." For example: *Le latin est une langue ancienne* means "Latin is an old language."

Adjective Placement

In French, most adjectives come after the noun. Some, however, come before the noun, while others vary depending on their meaning. Here are a few rules to remember:

- After the noun = color, shape, religion, nationality.

Examples

un thé vert	a green tea
un plat rond	a round plate
une église catholique	a Catholic church
une fille belge	a Belgian girl

- Before the noun = adjectives following the acronym BAGS (beauty, age, good/bad, size).

Examples

la belle femme	the beautiful woman
le jeune garçon	the young boy
le bon week-end	the good weekend
le petit chien	the little dog

- Some adjectives change meaning depending on their placement. The chart shows some common examples:

French adjective	Meaning before the noun	Meaning after the noun
brave	good	courageous
certain/certaine	particular	evident
cher/chère	dear	expensive
grand/grande	famous	tall
pauvre	poor (pitiful)	poor (not rich)
propre	one's own	clean
rare	few	of value

Activity A

Write the adjective in the correct place in the phrase.

1 la _____ fille _____ (belle)
2 le _____ chat _____ (petit)
3 la _____ voiture _____ (rouge)
4 le _____ livre _____ (américain)
5 la _____ table _____ (ronde)

Activity B

Choose the correct meaning of the adjective based on its location in the phrase.

1 l'ancien hôpital

   a the former hospital   **b the old hospital**

2 l'homme pauvre

   a the poor (not rich) man   **b the pitiful man**

3 la grande femme

   a the tall woman   **b the famous woman**

4 l'homme brave

   a the good man   **b the courageous man**

Your Turn

Now think of some other common adjectives. Look them up in a French-English Dictionary and use the rules to decide where to place them.

Qu'est-ce que vous faites ?

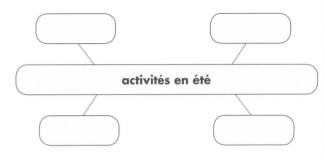

What are you doing?
Read this fact sheet
about Christophe Déry,
a famous soccer player.
Take a look to see what
Christophe likes to do
and wear for each season.

Nom Christophe Déry
Age 33 ans
Nationalité Canadien
Profession footballeur
Activités préférées
courir jouer au football voyager nager

Entretien (Interview)

Journaliste Qu'est-ce que vous faites d'habitude en été ?

Christophe En été, je joue au football, je nage et je cours.

Journaliste Vous ne voyagez pas en été ?

Christophe Si, je voyage souvent en été. C'est amusant. En hiver, je suis au Canada, et en été, je voyage un peu en Asie.

Journaliste En été, on n'a pas besoin de beaucoup de vêtements : seulement de sandales, de shorts, etc. Mais en hiver…

Christophe Vous avez raison. En hiver, il fait froid au Canada et je porte un blouson, une écharpe, des gants et des bottes.

Journaliste Regardez cette photo. C'est une photo de vous au Canada avec votre famille. Que faites-vous ?

Christophe Nous jouons dans la neige.

Activity A

Complete the word web with the activities Christophe does in the summer.

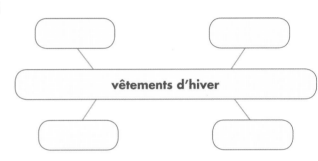

activités en été

Complete the word web with the clothing Christophe wears in the winter.

vêtements d'hiver

Activity B

Complete the following sentences about Christophe.

1 Christophe swims, runs and _____ in the summer.

2 Christophe travels in the _____.

3 Christophe wears a jacket in the _____.

4 Christophe is from _____ and is ____ years old.

CULTURE TIP

While *le football* is the French term for "soccer," don't confuse it with *le football américain* (football).

Smart Phrases

Core Phrases

C'est amusant.	It's fun.
C'est ennuyant.	It's boring.
D'habitude, en hiver, je fais ___.	In the winter, I usually ___.
Qu'est-ce que vous faites ?	What are you doing?
Qu'est-ce que vous faites d'habitude ?	What do you usually do?
Vous avez raison.	You're right.

Activity A

Qu'en pensez-vous ? (What do you think?) Write *C'est ennuyant* or *C'est amusant* to indicate what you think about each activity.

1 _____

2 _____

3 _____

4 _____

Activity B

What do you say if you want to...

1   ...ask someone what he or she is doing?

_____

2   ...ask someone what he or she usually does?

_____

3   ...tell what you usually do in the winter.

_____

4   ...tell someone he or she is right?

_____

Your Turn

Create a brief conversation between two friends, Amélie and Gerard, about an activity Gerard usually does in the winter. Have Amélie ask Gerard what he does and tell whether it's fun or boring. Then have Amélie say he's right. Use the interview with Christophe Déry in lesson 5 for help.

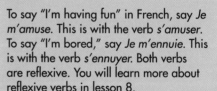

SMART TIP

To say "I'm having fun" in French, say *Je m'amuse.* This is with the verb *s'amuser.* To say "I'm bored," say *Je m'ennuie.* This is with the verb *s'ennuyer.* Both verbs are reflexive. You will learn more about reflexive verbs in lesson 8.

Words to Know

Core Words

Les vêtements (Clothing)

les bottes	boots (f)
le blouson	jacket
le chapeau	hat
les gants	gloves (m)
les sandales	sandals (f)

Les saisons (Seasons)

l'automne	autumn (m)
l'été	summer (m)
l'hiver	winter (m)
le printemps	spring (m)

Extra Words

courir	to run
jouer	to play
nager	to swim
porter	to wear
voyager	to travel

Activity B

Write the French word for each picture.

1 _____

2 _____

3 _____

SMART TIP

To say you do something during a particular season, place a preposition before the name of the season. To say "in summer," "in winter" or "in autumn," say *en été, en hiver* or *en automne*. To say "in spring," use *au* instead of *en*: *au printemps*.

Activity B

Use the words in the box to name the season in each picture.

> l'hiver   le printemps   l'été   l'automne

1 _____

2 _____

3 _____

4 _____

Activity C

Write the French word to complete each sentence.

1 Je porte _____ au printemps.
   _{a hat}

2 Elle porte _____ en automne.
   a jacket

3 Tu portes _____ en été.
   sandals

4 Ils portent _____ en hiver.
   gloves

Smart Grammar

Reflexive Verbs

- *Se laver* (to wash oneself) and *s'habiller* (to get dressed) are reflexive verbs. Reflexive verbs are for actions a person does to, at or for himself or herself.

- To form reflexive verbs, place the reflexive pronoun before the verb and follow the regular conjugation pattern. The pronoun agrees with the subject.

Reflexive Pronouns

je	**me**	myself
tu	**te**	yourself
il/elle	**se**	himself/herself
nous	**nous**	ourselves
vous	**vous**	yourselves
ils/elles	**se**	themselves

Se laver (to wash oneself)

je	**me** lave	I wash myself
tu	**te** laves	you wash yourself
il/elle	**se** lave	he/she washes himself/herself
nous	**nous** lavons	we wash ourselves
vous	**vous** lavez	you wash yourselves
ils/elles	**se** lavent	they wash themselves

- Other common reflexive verbs are *se réveiller* (to wake up), *se lever* (to get up), *se raser* (to shave) and *se coucher* (to go to bed).

- When referring to multiple people, the use of reflexive verbs can indicate that people are performing the action together. For example: *Ils se parlent* means "They speak to each other."

Activity A

Write a sentence in French telling what the following people do in the morning.

1 (Marie, se lever) _____

2 (nous, s'habiller) _____

3 (tu, se réveiller) _____

4 (ils, se raser) _____

Activity B

Conjugate the reflexive verb to say what people do together.

1  se marier

_____

2  s'embrasser

_____

3  se parler

_____

4 se téléphoner

_____

SMART TIP

Like the definite articles *le* and *la*, the reflexive pronouns *me, te* and *se* change in front of a vowel or silent h. They become *m', t'* and *s'* respectively. For example, *Il s'habille* (He gets dressed or He dresses himself).

Activity A

Circle the correct meaning for each phrase based on the placement of the adjective.

1 un livre cher

a a dear book   **b an expensive book**

2 ma propre maison

a my own house   **b my clean house**

3 un garçon brave

a a good boy   **b a courageous boy**

4 une grande femme

a a tall woman   **b a famous woman**

5 un ancien étudiant

a a former student   **b an old student**

Activity B

Write the French adjective in the correct place.

1 le _____ chat _____ (gris)
2 la _____ maison _____ (belle)
3 un _____ travail _____ (bon)
4 un _____ homme _____ (africain)
5 une _____ fille _____ (jeune)

Activity C

Quel temps fait-il ? (What's the weather like?) Sabine is going out, but before leaving she checks the weather report. Write in French what each image tells her about today's weather.

 1 _____

 2 _____

 3 _____

Activity D

Complete the word search to find words and phrases related to the weather and seasons.

soleil	chaud	froid	température	été
hiver	automne	vent	printemps	pluie

```
S O L E I L Z S C S H K W Y J
X Ç L A C H A Q H I V E R V V
E H H R W K M Q A Z K W X P L
H D A N J V R A U T O M N E J
Q P Y C X Q Z M D D Y D P Y Ç
F D S L A P R I M A V É R A V
X D O B M N A B R Z E K P E E
Q A L F L M S O L E A D O I N
F P R I N T E M P S A T U R T
P L Z Z Q G A L Q A W P E H R
U U S T A C A L I D O D L L F
A I J U G A R È G F R O I D W
B E V F É R H V R E P J U O D
S Q W R T P K A P P J R N Y U
T E M P É R A T U R E L Q X N
```

Challenge

You've already learned the formation and use of reflexive verbs in French. Now use those verbs to make a list of the things you do to get ready in the morning.

Internet Activity

Wonder what the weather is like in other countries? Go to **www.berlitzbooks.com/5minute** for a list of sites in French to browse. Find out what's happening right now in Paris. What about Montréal and Fort-de-France? Say *Où est-ce qu'il pleut maintenant ?* (Where is it raining right now?) *Quelle température fait-il ?* (What's the temperature?) *Quel temps fait-il ?* (What's the weather like?) *Est-ce qu'il fait chaud/froid ?* (Is it hot/cold?)

Unit 7 **Shopping**

In this unit you will:
- learn vocabulary related to shopping and payment.
- ask for pieces of clothing and sizes.
- make comparisons with *plus...que* (more than) and *moins...que* (less than).
- learn the irregular verb *mettre* (to put, to put on) and the regular verbs *s'habiller* (to dress oneself) and *porter* (to wear).

LESSON 1
Le magasin de vêtements

Dialogue

Adèle is at *un magasin de vêtements* (a clothing store). She is looking for a dress. Listen as she talks to *le vendeur* (the shop assistant).

Vendeur Bonjour. Je peux vous aider ?

Adèle Je cherche une robe.

Vendeur Les robes sont ici. Quelle taille recherchez-vous ?

Adèle Une taille moyenne, s'il vous plaît.

Vendeur De quelle couleur désirez-vous la robe ?

Adèle Je voudrais une robe bleue.

Activity A

Circle the correct picture.

1 Which item is Adèle looking for?

a   b   c

2 What dress size does Adèle want?

a  b  c

3 What color dress does Adèle want?

a   b   c

Activity B

Match the French questions with their English translations.

1 Je peux vous aider ?
   a **How can I help you?**
   b **How would you like to pay?**

2 Quelle taille recherchez-vous ?
   a **What color would you like?**
   b **What size do you need?**

3 De quelle couleur désirez-vous la robe ?
   a **What color dress would you like?**
   b **What size dress do you want?**

LESSON 2

Smart Phrases

Core Phrases

Ce _____ est trop grand/petit/serré/large.	This _____ is too large/small/tight/loose.
Je peux vous aider ?	How can I help you?
Je cherche _____.	I'm looking for _____.
Je cherche une taille _____.	I need a size _____.
Je voudrais acheter un/une _____.	I want to buy a _____.
Quelle taille recherchez-vous ?	What size do you need?
Vous désirez autre chose ?	Anything else?

Activity A

Choose the best response.

1 Bonjour. Je peux vous aider ?

a Je cherche une robe.
b La robe est trop petite.

2 Quelle taille recherchez-vous ?

a Une taille moyenne, s'il vous plaît.
b Je voudrais acheter une chemise.

3 Cette chemise est trop serrée.

a Je cherche un jean.
b Quelle taille recherchez-vous ?

4 Vous désirez autre chose ?

a Non, merci.
b La robe est trop large.

Activity B

Use one of the phrases you've learned to respond.

1 Je peux vous aider ?

_____.

Say that you are looking for a dress.

2 Vous désirez autre chose ?

_____.

Say that you need a medium shirt.

3 Vous désirez autre chose ?

_____.

Say that the blouse is too loose on you.

4 Quelle taille recherchez-vous ?

_____.

Say that you need a small.

> **SMART TIP**
>
> The word *autre* is very versatile. While in English we usually use "something" in statements and "anything" in questions, in French, *autre* is used for both. So, if someone asks *Vous désirez autre chose ?* (Do you want anything else?) you can respond *Oui, je voudrais autre chose* (Yes, I'd like something else).

LESSON 3

Words to Know

Core Words

Les vêtements (Clothing)

les chaussures	shoes (f)
la chemise	shirt
le chemisier	blouse
la cravate	tie
la jupe	skirt
le manteau	coat
le pantalon	pants
la robe	dress
le tee-shirt	T-shirt

Les tailles (Sizes)

petit/petite	small (m/f)
moyen/moyenne	medium (m/f)
grand/grande	large (m/f)
extra large	extra large

Couleurs (Colors)

blanc/blanche	white (m/f)
bleu/bleue	blue (m/f)
jaune	yellow
marron	brown
noir/noire	black (m/f)
rose	pink
rouge	red
vert/verte	green (m/f)
violet/violette	purple (m/f)

Activity A

Label the clothing in French.

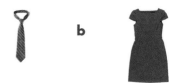

1 _____

2 _____

3 _____

4 _____

5 _____

Activity B

Read each sentence, then circle the item you are looking for.

1 Je cherche un chemisier rose.

a   b

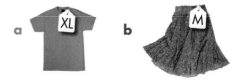

2 Je cherche une cravate rouge.

a   b

3 Je cherche un tee-shirt extra large.

a   b

4 Je cherche un manteau noir.

a   b

CULTURE TIP

In French, *le pantalon* (pants) is a singular noun, as opposed to the English word, which is plural. The same goes for "jeans"—*le jean*.

SMART TIP

In French-speaking countries the English abbreviations S, M, L and XL are used to mark the clothing sizes *petit*, *moyen*, *grand* and *extra large*.

Smart Grammar

To Dress, to Wear, to Put On

- *S'habiller* (to dress oneself) is a reflexive verb. It is conjugated as a regular *–er* verb.

- *Porter* (to wear) is a regular *–er* verb.

- *Mettre* (to put on) is an irregular *–re* verb. Look at the chart below for the conjugation.

je	mets	I put (on)
tu	mets	you put (on)
il/elle	met	he/she puts (on)
nous	mettons	we put (on)
vous	mettez	you put (on)
ils/elles	mettent	they put (on)

Examples

Je m'habille le matin.	I get dressed (literally, dress myself) in the morning.
Elle s'habille l'après-midi.	She gets dressed in the afternoon.
Je porte une chemise verte.	I'm wearing a green shirt.
Elle porte une robe bleue.	She's wearing a blue dress.
Je mets mon pantalon.	I put on my pants.
Il met ses chaussures.	He puts on his shoes.

SMART TIP

If you want to try something on in a store, use the verb *essayer* (to try). Example: *Puis-je essayer cette chemise ?* (Can I try on this shirt?). Ask for the *cabine d'essayage* (dressing room).

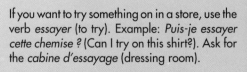

Activity A

Fill in the blanks with the correct verb.

1 Le matin, je _____.
   dress

2 Elle _____ une robe au travail.
   put on

3 Il _____ un manteau avant de quitter la maison.
   put on

4 Tu _____ une belle chemise aujourd'hui !
   wear

Activity B

Choose the correct conjugation of the verb *mettre* to complete each sentence.

1 Vous _____ une chemise le matin.

2 Tu _____ tes chaussures avant de quitter la maison.

3 Je _____ mon tee-shirt et mon pantalon.

4 Nous _____ nos chaussettes blanches.

5 Mes parents _____ leurs manteaux noirs chaque soir.

Activity C

Complete the conjugation chart for the reflexive verb *s'habiller*. Some are done for you. If you're not sure, look at the answer key in the back of the book.

je	m'	
tu	t'	habilles
il/elle/on	s'	
nous	nous	
vous	vous	habillez
ils/elles	s'	

SMART TIP

In France, major stores and retailers have sales twice a year in a nation-wide event called *les soldes*. They take place in January and in June and last for about two weeks. During *les soldes* the French government requires stores to put everything on sale to make room for the next season's merchandise. You'll find reductions anywhere from 10% to 80% off the original price.

How Will You Pay?

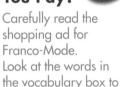

Carefully read the shopping ad for Franco-Mode. Look at the words in the vocabulary box to help you.

Franco-Mode

Venez à Franco-Mode pour les soldes d'été ! Jusqu'à 50% de remise sur les vêtements de chez B&M. Oui, cinquante pour cent ! Des vêtements très bon marché pour un maximum d'élégance ! 30 % de réduction sur les robes de chez Camille et Carmen. Inutile de payer cher pour être chic et à la mode !

Est-ce que c'est un prix hors taxe ?

Non, toutes les taxes sont comprises. Nous n'acceptons pas les cartes de crédit ou les cartes bancaires.

Now look at the ad for La Mode Parisienne. Note the differences between this ad and the previous one.

La Mode Parisienne

Venez à La Mode Parisienne pour les soldes d'été ! Bénéficiez de 20% de réduction sur les vêtements de B&M. Des vêtements très bon marché pour un maximum d'élégance !

40% sur les robes de Camille et Carmen. Il n'y a pas besoin de payer cher pour rester à la mode !

Est-ce que toutes les taxes sont comprises ?

Non, c'est un prix hors taxe. Nous acceptons les cartes de crédit et les cartes bancaires.

---

toutes taxes comprises (TTC)	all taxes included		
hors taxes (HT)	before taxes	Venez !	Come!
une robe de marque	designer dress	après	after
50% de réduction	50% off	avant	before
des soldes	sale	la taxe	sales tax

Activity A

Circle the correct answer. Use the ad to help you.

1 Which brand is in the ad?

  a Camille et Carmen   **b Laurent**

2 Are the dresses cheap or expensive?

  a cheap   **b expensive**

3 Are the prices with or without tax included?

  a with   **b without**

4 Does Franco-Mode accept credit or debit cards?

  a yes   **b no**

Activity B

Compare the ads and circle the correct answer.

1 At which store is the discount on B&M dresses greater?

  a Franco-Mode   **b La Mode Parisienne**

2 At which store is the discount on Camille et Carmen dresses greater?

  a Franco-Mode   **b La Mode Parisienne**

3 Are the prices at La Mode Parisienne with or without the taxes included?

  a with   **b without**

4 Does La Mode Parisienne take credit cards?

  a yes   **b no**

CULTURE TIP

The *dollar canadien* is the Canadian currency. The plural form is *dollars canadiens*. In France and Belgium the currency is the *euro* (€). Other currencies in the French-speaking world include the Swiss *franc* and the *franc CFA*, which is used in some central and western African countries.

LESSON 6

Smart Phrases

Core Phrases

Acceptez-vous les cartes de crédit et les cartes bancaires/chèques ?	Do you accept credit and debit cards/checks?
Ce n'est pas cher !	That's not expensive!
C'est bon marché !	It's cheap!
C'est trop cher !	That's too expensive!
Combien coûte ce pantalon ?	How much are these pants?
Combien coûte cette jupe ?	How much is this skirt?
Ils sont bon marché !	They're cheap!
Je paierai par carte de crédit.	I'll pay by credit card.
Oui, nous acceptons ____.	Yes, we accept ____.

Extra Phrases

Combien ça coûte TTC ?	How much does it cost with sales tax?
Je regarde seulement.	I'm just looking.
Je voudrais l'acheter.	I want to buy it.
Je voudrais les acheter.	I want to buy them.
Voici votre monnaie/reçu.	Here's your change/receipt.

Activity A

What do you say when you want to…

1 …ask if the shop accepts credit cards?

_____

2 …ask how much a skirt is?

_____

3 …ask if the shop accepts checks?

_____

4 …say you'll pay by credit card?

_____

5 …ask how much pants are?

_____

Activity B

Look at each picture and choose the word that best completes each statement.

> cher/chère (m/f)   bon marché

1

Elles sont _____.

2

Elle est _____.

3

Elle est _____.

4

Il est _____.

SMART TIP

In French it's common to use negative statements to express something positive. Example: saying *ce n'est pas cher* (it's not expensive) is the same as saying *c'est bon marché* (it's cheap). Keep in mind that in French you are likely to hear the negative form more than the positive.

LESSON 7

Words to Know

Core Words

l'argent	money
la carte bancaire	bank/debit card
la carte de crédit	credit card
le chèque	check
le dollar	dollar
en espèces	in cash
du liquide	cash
le reçu	receipt
une taxe	sales tax

Extra Words

les centimes	cents
la monnaie	change
la pièce	coin
le portefeuille	wallet

Activity A

Complete the sentences with the appropriate French word.

1 Acceptez-vous les _____ ?
   checks

3 Voici votre _____ .
   receipt

Activity B

Fill in the blanks with the correct French words to complete Jacques' thought bubble. Use the English translations as clues.

J'ai 500 euros en _____ dans mon
                        cash
portefeuille. J'ai aussi une _____ .
                              credit card
Je vais acheter beaucoup de vêtements parce

qu'il n'y a pas de _____ .
                        tax

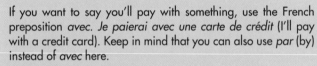

SMART TIP

If you want to say you'll pay with something, use the French preposition *avec*. *Je paierai avec une carte de crédit* (I'll pay with a credit card). Keep in mind that you can also use *par* (by) instead of *avec* here.

Je paierai par carte de crédit.   I'll pay by credit card.

If you want to say you'll pay in cash, use the French preposition *en*.

Je paierai en espèces.   I'll pay in cash.

2 Je paierai par _____ .
   credit card

4 Je n'ai pas d' _____ .
   money

Smart Grammar

Plus...que (more than) and moins...que (less than)

The phrases *plus...que* and *moins...que* are used to make comparisons. They're used the same way as their English equivalents.

J'ai plus d'argent que Julien.	I have more money than Julien.
Julien a moins d'argent que moi.	Julien has less money than I do.
Le manteau coûte plus que la cravate.	The coat costs more than the tie.
La cravate coûte moins que le manteau.	The tie costs less than the coat.

Activity A

Look at the items on the rack, then decide which items cost more and which cost less. Write *plus que* or *moins que* in the blanks to complete the sentences.

1 La robe coûte _____ le chemisier.

2 Le pantalon coûte _____ le manteau.

3 Le manteau coûte _____ la robe.

4 Le chemisier coûte _____ le pantalon.

Indefinite Pronouns

Indefinite pronouns are used when talking about an unspecified noun. There are many indefinite pronouns in French. Here are a few:

quelqu'un	someone, somebody, anyone or anybody
Example	Je connais quelqu'un qui vit au Canada. I know someone who lives in Canada.
quelque chose	something
Example	Je cherche quelque chose de bien. I'm looking for something nice.
quelques	some (people or things)
Example	J'ai besoin de quelques pièces. I need some coins.
personne	no one, nobody, none
Example	Personne ici ne mange de viande. Nobody here eats meat.
rien	nothing
Example	Il n'y a rien ici. There is nothing here.
tout	everything
Example	Tout est en solde. Everything is on sale.

Activity B

Circle the correct indefinite pronoun for each sentence.

1 **Quelqu'un/Quelque chose** veut manger ?

2 **Personne/Rien** ici n'étudie le français.

3 **Quelques/Quelque chose** robes sont bleues.

4 Tu veux **quelque chose/quelques** à manger ?

€100

€45

€20

€60

Activity A

As you've learned, *s'habiller*, *porter* and *mettre* have different meanings when it comes to wearing clothes. Choose the correct verb for each case in the sentences below.

1 Aujourd'hui, je **porte/mets** une robe.

2 Elles **s'habillent/mettent** leurs robes bleues.

3 Nous **portons/nous habillons** des tee-shirts aujourd'hui.

4 Le matin, il **s'habille/met**.

Challenge

Mettre (to put, to put on) is an important irregular verb. Try to complete the conjugation chart. Some are done for you, so pay attention to the pattern you see. If you are stuck, check the answer key for help.

je	
tu	mets
il/elle	
nous	
vous	mettez
ils/elles	

Activity B

Conjugate the verb *coûter* and tell which items are more and less expensive. Write two sentences for each pair, one with *plus que* and another with *moins que*.

Activity C

Based on the images, complete the crossword puzzle using the correct French word.

ACROSS	DOWN
1	1
2	3
4	
5 **S**	
6	

Internet Activity

Go to **www.berlitzbooks.com/5minute** for a list of French-language online shops to browse. Navigate each site in French and look at what is featured. Some sites may have different pages for *Hommes* and *Femmes*. What is your favorite *chemise*? What is your favorite *manteau*? If you don't mind international shipping fees, go ahead and make a purchase!

Unit 8 Travel and Holidays

In this unit you will:

- ask for directions.
- talk about location.
- discuss an itinerary.
- use the irregular verbs *aller* (to go) and *connaître* (to know a person or place).

Où est la gare ?

Dialogue

A couple from Canada is visiting Paris. They are looking for directions to the tourist office in *le Quartier Latin*. Listen as Guillaume and Lisette discuss where to go.

Lisette Nous sommes ici, sur la place du Parvis Notre-Dame. Comment faire pour aller à l'office de tourisme ?

Guillaume Regardons la carte. La place du Parvis Notre-Dame est au centre de Paris. Je voudrais prendre l'autobus ou le métro.

Lisette Mais nous ne sommes pas loin du Quartier Latin. Allons-y à pied !

Guillaume Mais le métro est près d'ici. C'est juste devant l'école.

Lisette Non, c'est mieux d'y aller à pied. Ainsi, nous pouvons mieux connaître les rues et les bâtiments de Paris. Je veux voir la bibliothèque et les vieilles églises.

Guillaume D'accord. Allons-y !

SMART TIPS

- *Allons-y !* is a common French phrase. It means "Let's go!"
- You can use the *nous* form of a verb to encourage someone to do something with you. For example: *Demandons-lui comment y aller* (Let's ask him for directions/Let's ask how to get there) or *Achetons un guide* (Let's buy a guide).
- *Y* can be used to replace the name of a place.

Activity A

Look at the clues. Try to guess the meaning of the following verbs. Write the English verb on the line.

1 arriver _____

2 prendre _____

3 marcher _____

Activity B

Answer the following questions in French. If you don't know a word, try to figure out the meaning through the context of the dialogue, then look at the Words to Know page to check your vocabulary.

1 Where are Guillaume and Lisette? _____

2 Where do they want to go? _____

3 What are the different options they have to get there? _____

4 Why does Lisette want to walk? _____

Activity A

Label each building, station or stop with the correct French word.

library

subway station

school

church

train station

bus stop

post office

supermarket

Core Words

Endroits (Places)

l'arrêt d'autobus	bus stop (m)
la bibliothèque	library
l'école	school (f)
l'église	church (f)
la gare routière	train station
la poste	post office
la station de métro	subway station
le supermarché	supermarket

Localisation (Location)

à côté de	next to
le coin	corner
à droite	to the right
à gauche	to the left
derrière	behind
devant	in front of
loin de	far from
près de	near

Activity B

Circle the appropriate term to describe where each thing is located.

1 La station de métro est _____ de la bibliothèque.

    a à gauche   **b à droite**

2 L'école est _____ la gare routière.

    a loin de   **b près de**

3 Le supermarché est _____ la bibliothèque.

    a loin de   **b près de**

4 La station de métro est _____ l'école.

    a loin de   **b à côté de**

SMART TIP

To indicate that something is to the left or right of something else, use the preposition *à* before *gauche* or *droite*. *La bibliothèque est à gauche de l'école* (The library is to the left of the school).

Smart Phrases

Core Phrases

Achetons une carte.	Let's buy a map.
Où est _____ ?	Where is _____?
Comment vais-je à _____ ?	How do I get to _____?
Je veux prendre le train/l'autobus /le métro.	I want to take the train/bus/subway.
La gare est près de l'église.	The train station is near the church.

Extra Phrases

Excusez-moi.	Excuse me.
Merci./Merci bien./ Merci beaucoup.	Thank you./Thanks a lot./ Thank you very much.
De rien.	You're welcome.

Activity A

Look at each picture. Write in French that you want to use that mode of transport. Then ask where you can find the station or stop.

1

Je veux prendre_____.

Où est_____ ?

2

_____

_____

3

_____

_____

Activity B

What do you say if you want to…

1 …ask where the train station is?

_____

_____

2 …ask how to get to the subway station?

_____

_____

3 …tell someone the train station is near the school?

_____

_____

4 …say "let's buy a map"?

_____

_____

Activity C

You are helping a tourist with directions to the Latin Quarter. To get there he has to take the bus to the church. The bus stop is behind the post office. Read his questions and tell him what to do.

1 Comment vais-je au Quartier Latin ?

_____

_____

_____

2 Comment vais-je à l'arrêt d'autobus ?

_____

_____

_____

Your Turn

You want to go to the bus station. Ask—out loud—where it is and how to get there. Don't forget to be polite!

LESSON 4
Smart Grammar

The verb *aller* (to go)

The verb *aller* is irregular. The chart shows its conjugation in the present tense.

je	vais	I go
tu	vas	you go
il/elle	va	he/she goes
nous	allons	we go
vous	allez	you go
ils/elles	vont	they go

Examples

Je vais à l'école. I go to school.
Nous allons au supermarché. We go to the supermarket.

Activity A

Fill in the blanks with the correct form of *aller*.

1 Elles _____ à la bibliothèque.
2 Elle _____ à l'église.
3 Nous _____ au poste.
4 Tu _____ à la gare.

Activity B

Choose the correct conjugation of *aller* to complete the questions.

1 _____-vous à la poste ?
2 Comment _____-je au train ?
3 Est-ce qu'ils _____ à l'eglise ?
4 Où _____-vous ?

Activity C

Write sentences with the verb *aller* to tell where you think someone will go. Remember to use the contractions *à la* and *au* when needed.

1 Ils _____
_____
_____

2 Nous _____
_____
_____

3 Elles _____
_____
_____

4 Vous _____
_____
_____

CULTURE TIP

If you are traveling from city to city in France, airfare can be expensive. A good alternative between big cities is the train system. It's reliable, fast and easy. You may even make some friends along the way. All trains are operated by the national railroad company, SNCF. The TGV (*le train à grande vitesse*) is the fastest high-speed commercial train in the world, going from Calais to Marseille in just three and a half hours!

Arrivées et départs

Arrivals and Departures

Read the e-mail from Dylan to Henri with information about their trip to Brussels.

```
○ ○ ○
Date :    mardi, le 26 avril
De :      Dylan
À :       Henri
Sujet :   Bruxelles

Salut Henri !
Finalement, je pars en vacances ! Je
vais à Bruxelles !
Tu connaîs Bruxelles ? Moi, je ne
connaîs pas.
J'ai les billets d'avion et une
réservation d'hôtel. Ma valise est déjà
faite.
Voici les informations : le numéro du
vol est le 12-35. Je vais de New York à
Bruxelles. L'avion part de New York à
20h et arrive à Bruxelles le lendemain
à midi.
De l'aéroport de Bruxelles, je vais en
autobus jusqu'à l'hôtel.
Nous nous voyons à l'hôtel.
À bientôt,
Dylan
```

SMART TIPS

- The preposition *de* can be used like its English equivalent, "from," when talking about going from place to place. But when referring to destinations use *à* (to): *Je vais de New York à Bruxelles* (I go from New York to Brussels).

- *Jusqu'à* means "until" or "as far as." *Je prends le bus jusqu'à l'hôtel* (I take the bus to the hotel. Literally: I take the bus as far as the hotel).

- *Déjà* means "already." *J'ai déjà les billets* (I already have the tickets).

Activity A

Circle the correct answer for each question.

1   Where are Dylan and Henri going?
    a New York   **b Brussels**

2   Do they have a hotel reservation?
    a yes   **b no**

3   What time does the plane leave New York?
    a 8 PM   **b 12 PM**

4   How are they getting to the hotel from the airport?
    a by bus   **b by subway**

Activity B

Dylan and Henri's flight itinerary has changed. Look at the new information and complete Dylan's e-mail.

Lufthansa Airlines			LF12-35
Departs	**Time**	**Arrives**	**Time**
New York JFK International Airport	10:00 PM	Brussels International Airport	2:00 PM

```
○ ○ ○
Date :    mercredi, le 27 avril
De :      Dylan
À :       Henri
Sujet :   Bruxelles

Bonjour Henri,
J'ai de nouvelles informations sur le
vol de demain. Le vol part de New York
à _____. Nous arrivons à
Bruxelles à _____.

Dylan
```

Words to Know

Core Words

l'aéroport	airport (m)
l'avion	plane (m)
le bagage	luggage
le billet	ticket
le passeport	passport
les vacances	holiday (f)
la valise	suitcase
le voyage	trip
le vol	flight

Extra Words

l'escale	stop/layover (f)
l'hôtel	hotel (m)
la réservation	reservation

Activity A

Pick the correct French term from the choices below.

1 luggage
   a **le bagage**   b **le passeport**   c **le billet**

2 flight
   a **le vol**   b **la valise**   c **l'avion**

3 trip
   a **les vacances**   b **le voyage**   c **le billet**

4 vacation
   a **le voyage**   b **les vacances**   c **le bagage**

Activity B

Draw a line to match each picture with the correct French word.

1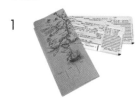

   a   le passeport

2

   b   le billet

3

   c   l'avion

4

   d   la valise

5

   e   l'aéroport

CULTURE TIP

Citizens of most English-speaking countries can visit France for up to 90 days with only a passport. But if you plan to stay longer you will need to apply for a *visa de long séjour* (long stay visa) and a *carte de séjour* (residence permit). There are strict rules for this type of permit, so you should research and prepare for the application process in advance.

Smart Phrases

Core Phrases

Quand est le prochain vol pour Bruxelles ?	When is the next flight to Brussels?
Quelle est la porte des départs ?	Which is the departure gate?
Quelle est la porte des arrivées ?	Which is the arrival gate?
Le vol part à ___.	The flight leaves at ___.
L'avion arrive à ___.	The plane arrives at ___.
Combien coûte le vol ?	How much does the flight cost?
Le vol coûte ___ euros aller-retour.	The flight costs ___ euros round-trip.

Extra Phrases

Enfin !	At last!
On se voit à _____.	I'll see you at _____.
À bientôt !	See you soon!

Activity A

What do you say if you want to…

1   …tell your friend that your flight leaves at 12:30 PM?

   _____

2   …ask which is the departing gate?

   _____

3   …ask which is the arriving gate?

   _____

4   …tell your friend that the plane arrives at 5:00 PM?

   _____

Activity B

Armand is looking for the next available flight to Geneva. He goes up to a ticket agent and asks him a few questions. Circle the best responses to Armand's questions.

1   Quand est le prochain vol pour Genève ?

   a Le vol part à 8h.   **b Le vol arrive à 12h.**

2   Bien. Je le prends. Quelle est la porte des départs ?

   a La porte A5.   **b Le vol part à 8h.**

3   Quelle est la porte des arrivées ?

   a L'avion arrive à 18h. **b La porte C19.**

Activity C

Look at the chart and answer the questions below.

Départ		
Heure	Destination	Vol
16:15	Lyon	EZY5258
16:35	Marseille	EZY5259
17:00	Toulouse	MZY448058
17:00	Paris	VZX7250
17:20	Strasbourg	VZX7251
17:25	Bordeaux	LNN4432

1   Quand est le prochain vol pour Toulouse ?

   _____

2   Quel vol part à 17h20 ?

   _____

Your Turn

You work for Air France and you have to announce the next flight to Paris: flight 1699, departs at 10:23 AM, arrives at 1:30 PM. Use your new phrases and vocabulary to give information about the flight.

SMART TIP

Aller-retour means "round-trip."
Aller-simple means "one-way."
"Business class" is *la classe affaires*, "first class" is *la première classe* and "economy class" is *la classe économique*.

Smart Grammar

The verb *connaître* (to know)

The verb *connaître* is irregular. The chart shows its conjugation in the present tense.

je	connais	I know
tu	connais	you know
il/elle	connaît	he/she knows
nous	connaissons	we know
vous	connaissez	you know
ils/elles	connaissent	they know

Examples

Je connais Thomas.	I know Thomas.
Elles connaissent Paris.	They know Paris.
Je ne connais pas Montréal.	I don't know Montreal.

SMART TIP

While the irregular French verb *connaître* literally translates as "to know," it usually means "to be familiar with," and it should be applied to people and places, not to facts, skills or ideas. The verb meaning "to know" for facts and ideas is *savoir*. For example:

Je sais nager.	I know how to swim.
Nous savons parler français.	We know how to speak French.
Julia sait qui vient.	Julia knows who is coming.

Activity A

Conjugate the verb *connaître* so that it makes sense in each sentence.

1 Est-ce que tu _____ New York ?

2 Je ne _____ pas le Québec.

3 Nous _____ la mère de Joseph.

4 Est-ce que vous _____ Muriel ?

Direct Object Pronouns

me	me
te	you (sing., inf.)
le	him/it (m)
la	her/it (f)
nous	us
vous	you (sing./pl., form.)
les	them

Examples

Armand me connaît.	Armand knows me.
Je connais Pierre.	I know Pierre.
Je le connais.	I know him.
Je vois la maison.	I see the house.
Je la vois.	I see it.

Activity B

Change the sentences so they use direct object pronouns.

1 Je prends le train. _____

2 Elle étudie le français. _____

3 Tu connais la maison. _____

4 Elles prennent les billets. _____

Your Turn

Do you know them? Look at each picture and write a sentence using *connaître* to indicate if you know or don't know each person, place or animal.

1  2

_____   _____

3  4

_____   _____

Activity A

Read Tristan's postcard from his trip to Canada. He didn't conjugate the verbs *aller* and *connaître* correctly. Cross out the mistakes and rewrite the verbs using the correct form.

Chère Claire,

Ma mère et moi sommes à Montréal. Demain, nous partons pour la ville de Québec. Tu connaît Québec ? Je le connaissez bien. Ensuite, nous vont à Halifax. Est-ce que tu connaissent Halifax ?

Bises,

Tristan
Robert

Ms. Rosa Seurat
Box 219
Anaheim, California
U. S. A.

Activity B

Fill in the blanks to complete Charlotte's plan for her trip to Lyon.

Mon voyage à Lyon

_____ à Lyon en France. _____
I go   My flight leaves at

8h du matin. J'arrive _____ à 6h
                                    at the airport

du matin. C'est si tôt ! J'ai mon _____,
                                                            ticket

ma _____ et mon _____. J'arrive à Lyon
      luggage   passport

à 10h du matin, et je cherche _____ pour aller
                                                  a bus

à l'hôtel. L'hôtel est _____ la Place Bellecour.
                                  near

Je le connais. Il est _____. Demain,
                              behind a church

_____ à l'Opéra National. J'ai
I want to take the subway

besoin d'un ticket de métro. Ah, je l'ai.

Activity C

Auguste and Véronique are looking for the post office. Write the correct French word or phrase to help complete their dialogue.

Auguste   Où est la poste ?

Véronique   _____ une carte.
                          Let's buy

Auguste   Regardons la carte. La poste est

_____.
to the right of the library

Véronique   Oui, et c'est aussi _____.
                                              behind the supermarket

Auguste   C'est _____.
                          the bus stop

Véronique   Oui. _____ le bus ici.
                          Let's take

Challenge

As you know, *savoir* also means "to know," but it's used with facts, ideas and knowing how to do things. *Savoir* is also irregular, but the conjugation follows similar verb rules as the ones you've already learned. Can you complete the chart?

je	sais
tu	
il/elle	
nous	
vous	savez
ils/elles	

Internet Activity

Go to **www.berlitzbooks.com/5minute** and look for sites in French that help you book the next available flight to Paris. Enter your city of *départ* (departure), your *destination* (destination city), your *date aller* (departure date) and your *date retour* (return date). Choose *classe économique* or *première classe* (economy class or first class) and hit *chercher*. Quand est le prochain vol pour Paris ? Combien coûte le vol ?

In this unit you will:
- describe different professions.
- compare different jobs.
- read a job application in French.
- conjugate regular verbs in the past and future tenses.

LESSON 1
Entretien de travail

Dialogue

Hélène is on a job interview for *Le Monde*, a famous newspaper. Listen as her potential employer asks about her previous job and responsibilities.

Employeur Où avez-vous travaillé ?

Hélène J'ai travaillé dans un journal, *Le Figaro*.

Employeur Avez-vous écrit des articles pour ce journal ?

Hélène Oui. J'ai écrit plusieurs articles pour ce journal.

Employeur Sur quels sujets avez-vous écrit ?

Hélène Sur la culture francophone. Voici les articles.

Employeur Ces articles sont très bien ! Vous êtes embauchée !

Hélène Merci beaucoup ! Quand est-ce que je commence ?

Employeur Lundi prochain. Je vous verrai lundi à 8h.

SMART PRONUNCIATION

There are two types of *h* in French: the *h muet* (mute h) and the *h aspiré* (aspirated h). Words of Latin or Greek origin beginning with *h* take the *h muet*. The *h* in these words is silent. For example: *l'hôpital* (hospital) = loh•pee•tahl, *l'homme* (man) = lohm. The *h aspiré* typically appears in words borrowed from languages other than Latin or Greek. The *h* in these words is pronounced. For example: *la honte* (shame) = lah hohnt, *la hache* (axe) = lah hahsh.

SMART TIPS

- *Sur* (on) can be used with the verb *porter* to talk about the topic or theme of a book, movie or article. Example: *L'article porte sur l'économie* (The article is about the economy).

- The verb *traiter* (to treat) with the preposition *de* can also be used. Example: *Le livre traite de la vie de Chamoiseau* (The book is about Chamoiseau's life).

Activity A

Circle the correct answer for each question.

1. Where did Hélène work last?
   - **a journal**
   - **b université**

2. What did Hélène do at her previous job?
   - **a enseigné**
   - **b écrit**

3. What does Hélène show the employer?
   - **a photos**
   - **b articles**

4. Does Hélène get the job?
   - **a oui**
   - **b non**

Activity B

Choose a word from the box to complete each sentence.

> a écrit   la culture   commencera   travaille

1. Hélène _____ dans un journal.

2. Hélène _____ des articles pour un journal.

3. Elle a écrit des articles sur _____.

4. Hélène _____ lundi à 8h.

Words to Know

Core Words

le bureau	office
l'étudiant/l'étudiante	student (m/f)
le journal	newspaper
le journaliste/la journaliste	journalist (m/f)
le magazine	magazine
le professeur	teacher
la profession	profession
la salle de classe	classroom
le travail	job
travailler	to work

Extra Words

l'article	article (m)
l'employeur/l'employeuse	employer (m/f)

SMART TIP

Unlike most French nouns, you cannot tell the gender of the word *journaliste* (journalist) by its ending. Instead, you should look at the article or the context. This is also true for the words *secrétaire* (secretary) and *artiste* (artist).

CULTURE TIP

In French, the word *journal* is not only used to refer to print newspapers. It's also used colloquially for televised news programs, or more formally *le journal télévisé*. Popular print newspapers in France are *Le Monde*, *Le Figaro* and *Libération*. Popular televised news programs can be found on TV5, TF1 and France 2.

Activity A

Fill in the blanks with the correct French word to complete Aurore's diary entry.

le 6 avril

Je suis dans une _____.
                    classroom

_____ me parle d'un article dans le journal.
The teacher

Il y a beaucoup d'_____ dans ma classe.
                    students

Je ne veux pas rester ici. Je veux travailler comme

_____ pour un _____
    journalist   newspaper

ou un _____. Je ne veux pas être
            magazine

_____.
    student

Activity B

Label each picture with the appropriate French word and its article.

a

b   c

a   Le Figaro

b   c

LESSON 3

Smart Phrases

Core Phrases

Quelle est votre profession ? — What is your profession?
Je suis journaliste. — I'm a journalist. (m/f)
Je suis professeur. — I'm a teacher. (m/f)
Qu'est-ce que vous voulez faire ? — What do you want to do?
Je veux être professeur. — I want to be a teacher.

Extra Phrases

Je vous verrai lundi. — I'll see you Monday.
Nous nous verrons lundi. — We'll see each other Monday.
Vous êtes embauché/embauchée. — You're hired. (m/f)

Activity A

Quelle est votre profession ? Look at the pictures and complete the sentences to tell the person's profession.

1 Je suis _____ 2 Je suis _____

Que'est-ce que vous voulez faire ? Now look at the pictures and decide what each person wants to be. Write the answer on the blanks below.

3 _____   4 _____

Activity B

What do you say when you want to…

1 …ask what someone wants to be?

_____

2 …say you want to be a teacher?

_____

3 …ask someone about his or her profession?

_____

4 …say you're a journalist?

_____

Your Turn

Imagine you're a journalist. You're meeting a professor for the first time. Tell her your current profession and ask about hers. Then use the words *créateur/créatrice de mode* (fashion designer), *écrivain/écrivaine* (writer) or *artiste* (artist) to tell her what you want to be.

Write your sentences for more practice.

_____

_____

_____

_____

_____

_____

_____

SMART TIP

When telling someone your profession in French, omit the article before the job name. Examples: *Je suis écrivain* (I'm a writer), *Je suis infirmière* (I'm a nurse).

Smart Grammar

Regular Verbs in the Past Tense

To form the past tense—or *passé composé*—of most regular verbs, use the present tense of *avoir* before the past participle of the main verb.

Verbs with –er

To form the past participle of regular –er verbs, drop the –er and add –é to the end, such as with *travailler* (to work).

j'	ai	travaill**é**	I worked
tu	as	travaill**é**	you worked
il/elle	a	travaill**é**	he/she worked
nous	avons	travaill**é**	we worked
vous	avez	travaill**é**	you worked
ils/elles	ont	travaill**é**	they worked

Verbs with –ir

To form the past participle of regular –ir verbs, drop the –ir and add –i to the end, such as with *finir* (to finish).

j'	ai	fin**i**	I finished
tu	as	fin**i**	you finished
il/elle	a	fin**i**	he/she finished
nous	avons	fin**i**	we finished
vous	avez	fin**i**	you finished
ils/elles	ont	fin**i**	they finished

Verbs with –re

To form the past participle of regular –re verbs, drop the –re and add –u to the end, such as with *vendre* (to sell).

j'	ai	vend**u**	I sold
tu	as	vend**u**	you sold
il/elle	a	vend**u**	he/she sold
nous	avons	vend**u**	we sold
vous	avez	vend**u**	you sold
ils/elles	ont	vend**u**	they sold

Activity A

Complete the sentences with the past tense of the verb.

1 Tu _____ huit heures
   travailler
   hier (yesterday).

2 Elle _____ beaucoup de livres le
   vendre
   mois dernier).

3 L'année dernière (last year), j'_____ le
   finir
   tableau (the painting).

4 Nous _____ au bureau la semaine
   travailler
   dernière (last week).

Activity B

Rewrite the following sentences in the past tense.

1 Je travaille au bureau.

   _____

2 Vous vendez des livres de français.

   _____

3 Elle habite en France.

   _____

4 Tu manges une salade.

   _____

5 Elle entend la question.

   _____

6 Marie et moi oublions de fermer la porte.

   _____

LESSON 5
Une demande d'emploi

A Job Application

Nicolas is applying for *un poste de correcteur* (proofreader position) at *Le Monde. Un jour* (some day) he wants to be a journalist. Look at his *formulaire de candidature* (application form), then answer the questions below.

Demande d'emploi pour Le Monde

Nicolas Delatour	*04 92 83 58 59*
Nom	Numero de téléphone
10, Place Saint-Claire, 16100 Cognac, France	
Adresse	

FORMATION :

Université	Spécialisation	de – à
la Sorbonne	*Journalisme*	*2005 – 2009*

EXPÉRIENCE PROFESSIONNELLE :

Crédit Lyonnais	*secrétaire*
Employeur	Poste
juin 2004 – septembre 2005	*Grégoire Durand*
de – à	Patron

Libération	*assistant éditorial*
Employeur	Poste
mai 2008 – présent	*Marie-Pascale Jennepin*
de – à	Patron

Dernier salaire : *€28.000*

Salaire souhaité : *€33.000*

Poste désiré : *correcteur*

Pourquoi désirez-vous ce poste ?
*Parce qu'un jour, je voudrais être journaliste.
À Libération, j'ai beaucoup appris. Comme
correcteur, j'apprendrai beaucoup plus.*

Activity A

Complete the sentences with information from the application.

1. Nicolas Delatour is applying for a position as

   _____.

2. He studied journalism at the Sorbonne for _____ years.

3. His first job was at _____.

4. From May 2008 to the present he has worked for

   _____.

5. He thinks he will learn more if he works for _____.

Activity B

The verb *souhaiter* (to wish, desire) is similar to *vouloir* (to want). Can you guess the meaning of these words?

1. poste souhaité _____

2. salaire souhaité _____

LESSON 6

Words to Know

Core Words

l'assistant/l'assistante	assistant (m/f)
l'employé/l'employée	employee (m/f)
le patron/la patronne	boss (m/f)
le secrétaire/la secrétaire	secretary (m/f)
le salaire	salary

Extra Words

les affaires	business
beaucoup (de)	a lot (of)
difficile	difficult
dur	hard
l'entreprise	company (f)
facile	easy
intéressant/intéressante	interesting (m/f)

Activity A

Circle the word that best answers each question.

1   Which word is not a type of job?

   a assistant   **b secrétaire**   **c salaire**

2   Which word doesn't change its ending in the feminine form?

   a assistant   **b patron**   **c secrétaire**

3   Which person pays your salary?

   a correcteur   **b patron**   **c assistant**

4   What do you call the amount of money you get paid for your work?

   a employé   **b salaire**   **c travail**

Activity B

Read the clues and complete the crossword puzzle.

Across

1   Une personne qui aide (helps). (m)

4   Paiement (payment) pour mon travail.

5   Cette personne paye mon salaire. (m)

6   Il travaille pour moi. C'est mon _____.

Down

2   Cette personne organise les choses dans le bureau.

3   Je suis journaliste. C'est mon _____.

Your Turn

Imagine you have your own *enterprise*. Create a list of the people you need to hire. How many *employés*? How many of those will be *assistants* and *secrétaires*? What is the *salaire* for each *employé*?

Smart Phrases

Core Phrases

Pourquoi désirez-vous ce poste ?	Why do you want this position?
Parce que je veux être journaliste.	Because I want to be a journalist.
J'aime aider.	I like to help.
J'aime écrire.	I like to write.
Pendant combien de temps y avez-vous travaillé ?	How long did you work there?
J'y ai travaillé pendant trois mois.	I worked there for three months.
C'est plus facile que ___.	It's easier than ___.
C'est plus difficile que ___.	It's harder than ___.

Extra Phrases

Il/Elle paye plus.	It pays more. (m/f)
Il/Elle paye moins.	It pays less. (m/f)

SMART TIPS

- To specify how long you worked or lived somewhere, use the words *pendant* (for) or *depuis* (since). *Pendant* may indicate that the action has ended, while *depuis* suggests that the action could still be going on. For example: *J'ai travaillé à Paris pendant huit ans* (I worked in Paris for eight years). *J'habite en France depuis deux mois* (I have been living in France for two months).

- To say what activities you like use *j'aime* and add a verb in the infinitive form. For example: *J'aime jouer* (I like to play), *J'aime chanter* (I like to sing), *J'aime lire* (I like to read).

Activity A

What do you think? Write *plus facile* or *plus difficile* to compare each pair of jobs.

1 Le travail d'un médecin est _____ que le travail d'un dentiste (dentist).

2 Le travail d'un professeur est _____ que le travail d'un ingénieur (engineer).

3 Le travail d'un journaliste est _____ que le travail d'un avocat (lawyer).

4 Le travail d'un secrétaire est _____ que le travail d'un créateur de mode (fashion designer).

Activity B

What do you say if you want to...

1 ...ask someone why he or she wants to be a journalist?

_____

_____

2 ...tell someone you like to help?

_____

_____

3 ...ask someone how long he or she worked somewhere?

_____

_____

4 ...tell someone that you worked somewhere for two years?

_____

_____

Regular Verbs in the Future Tense

To make the future tense of regular −er and −ir verbs, use the full infinitive plus the following endings:

je	travaillerai	I will work
tu	travailleras	you will work
il/elle	travaillera	he/she will work
nous	travaillerons	we will work
vous	travaillerez	you will work
ils/elles	travailleront	they will work

Examples

Nous ne travaillerons pas la semaine prochaine. — We will not work next week.

Quand est-ce que vous finirez le livre ? — When will you finish the book?

To form the future tense of regular −re verbs, drop the final e from the infinitive and add the same future endings as −er and −ir verbs.

je	vendrai	I will sell
tu	vendras	you will sell
il/elle	vendra	he/she will sell
nous	vendrons	we will sell
vous	vendrez	you will sell
ils/elles	vendront	they will sell

Example

Je vendrai plus demain. — I will sell more tomorrow.

Activity A

Complete the sentences by writing the future tense of each verb. Be sure to read the entire sentence for its context.

1 Qu'est-ce que tu _____ le vendredi ?
   étudier

2 Je _____ dans la salle de classe plus tard.
   travailler

3 Elles _____ une carte postale demain.
   écrire

4 Lundi, nous _____ au bureau.
   travailler

Activity B

This is Laure's wish list for next year. Use the future tense to tell what she will do.

1 étudier le chinois
   _____

2 aider ma famille
   _____

3 rendre visite à mes cousins
   _____

4 lire un livre de Proust
   _____

5 corriger ma thèse (thesis)
   _____

6 voyager une fois par mois (once a month)
   _____

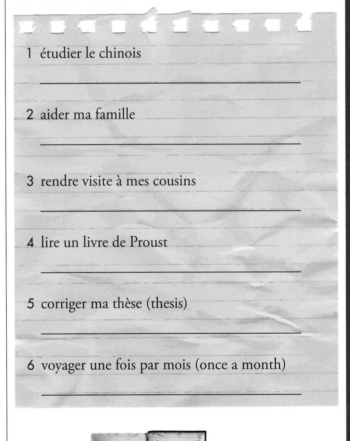

Review

Activity A

Use the clues to complete the crossword puzzle.

ACROSS	DOWN
3 difficult	1 student (m)
5 teacher (m)	2 secretary (m)
	4 easy

Activity B

Complete the missing question for each exchange. Use the correct past or future conjugation for each verb.

1 Quand _____ ?
  Elles travailleront samedi prochain.

2 Quand _____ ?
  J'ai fini le livre samedi dernier.

3 Quand _____ ?
  Elle vendra plus de livres la semaine prochaine.

Activity C

Now write the missing question or answer in each exchange.

1 Quand est-ce que Marie travaillera au bureau ?
  _____

2 Quand est-ce que tu as vendu le DVD ?
  _____

3 Elle visitera le Royaume-Uni en avril.
  _____

4 Nous avons mangé une pizza pour le déjeuner.
  _____

Activity D

Each of the following sentences contains a misspelled word. Rewrite the sentences to correct the mistakes.

1 Quel est ton travaille ?
  _____

2 Pour qui est-ce que tu travaillez ?
  _____

3 Quel salary souhaites-tu ?
  _____

4 Quand est-ce qu'ils finira le livre ?
  _____

> ### Challenge
> What is another French word for *difficile* ? _____
>
> What is another French word for *vouloir* ? _____

Internet Activity

Looking for a job? Go to **www.berlitzbooks.com/5minute** for a list of French-language job search engines to browse. How many *assistant/assistante* positions can you find? What about *secrétaires* and *professeurs*? What are the *salaires* like for each position?

In this unit you will:

• talk about things to do around a house or an apartment.
• use commands to give orders and instructions.
• use expressions for going out at night.
• use vocabulary about places to go.
• learn the past tense of the verbs *aller* and *être*.

LESSON 1

Aide-moi !

Eve's E-mail

Eve writes an e-mail to her brother David. She asks him to help her clean her apartment. (Notice how they are using the informal because they are related.)

```
⊖ ○ ○
Date :    mardi, le 26 avril
De :      Eve
À :       David
Sujet :   Aide-moi !

Bonjour David,
Peux-tu m'aider à ranger mon
appartement ? Papa et maman arriveront
demain et l'appartement est en
désordre. Je veux d'abord ramasser les
vêtements et ranger le placard de la
salle de bain. Ensuite, je veux nettoyer
le sol et repeindre ma chambre.
Comment peux-tu m'aider ? Tu ramasses
les vêtements et je range le placard.
Puis, nous nettoyons le sol et
repeignons les murs ensemble.
Aide-moi, s'il te plaît !
Bisous,
Eve
```

en désordre	messy	peindre	to paint
ramasser	to pick up	repeindre	to repaint
nettoyer	to clean	ensemble	together
Ne t'inquiète pas.	Don't worry.		

Activity A

Circle the correct answer for each question.

1   What does Eve need help with?
    a her house   **b her apartment**

2   Who will visit Eve tomorrow?
    a her parents   **b her aunt and uncle**

3   What does Eve ask David to do?
    a organize her closet **b pick up her clothes**

4   What does Eve suggest they do together?
    a organize   **b paint**

David's Response

```
⊖ ○ ○
Date :    mardi, le 26 avril
De :      David
À :       Eve
Sujet :   Aide-moi !

Bonjour Eve,
Oui, je peux t'aider. Mais je ne veux pas
ramasser tes vêtements. Tu ramasses tes
vêtements et je range le placard. Puis,
nous nettoyons et repeignons ensemble.
Ne t'inquiète pas. Je t'aiderai.
À bientôt,
David
```

Activity B

Read David's response and answer each question in French.

1   Is David going to help Eve?

_____

2   What doesn't David want to do?

_____

3   What does David want to do?

_____

4   What does David say that Eve and he can do together?

_____

Words to Know

Core Words

l'appartement	apartment (m)
la chambre	bedroom
la cuisine	kitchen
les pièces	rooms (f)
le placard	closet
la salle à manger	dining room
la salle de bain	bathroom
la salle de séjour	living room

Extra Words

les escaliers	stairs (m)
la fenêtre	window
le jardin	garden
le sol	floor

Activity A

Fill in the blanks with the correct French word to complete the dialogue. For the *moi* part of the dialogue, answer the questions based on your own home.

Ami Est-ce que tu habites dans une maison ou _____ ?
                  an apartment

Moi J'habite dans _____ .

Ami Combien de _____ y a-t-il ?
                rooms

Moi Il y a _____ .

Ami Quelles sont _____ les plus grandes ?
                the rooms

Moi Il y a la/les _____ , la salle à manger,
                bedroom(s)
la cuisine et la salle de séjour.

Activity B

Look at each picture. Then choose the correct word from the box to name each picture.

> la salle de bain   la chambre   la cuisine
> la salle à manger   le placard   la salle de séjour

1 _____

2 _____

3 _____

4 _____

5 _____

6 _____

CULTURE TIP

In France, *la salle de bain* is often a separate room from *les toilettes*. In *la salle de bain*, you'll find a shower, a bathtub and a sink. In *les toilettes*, you will find a toilet and, in some cases, a sink.

Smart Phrases

Core Phrases

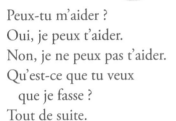

Peux-tu m'aider ?	Can you help me?
Oui, je peux t'aider.	Yes, I can help you.
Non, je ne peux pas t'aider.	No, I can't help you.
Qu'est-ce que tu veux que je fasse ?	What do you want me to do?
Tout de suite.	Right away.

Extra Phrases

Aide-moi s'il te plaît !	Help me please!
Donne-moi un coup de main.	Give me a hand.
À bientôt.	See you soon.
bisous	kisses

SMART TIP

Did you notice the informal was used in the phrases above? That's because the correspondence in Lesson 1 was between siblings. Remember to use the formal when speaking to all but family, friends and children. If you were asking for help at a store, you would say *Pouvez-vous m'aider ?* rather than *Peux-tu m'aider ?*

Activity A

What do you say if you want to…

1 …ask someone to help you?

_____

2 …say that you can't help someone?

_____

3 …ask what someone wants you to do?

_____

4 …say "right away"?

_____

Activity B

Put the dialogue in order. Number the phrases 1–4.

> Oui, je peux t'aider. Qu'est-ce que tu veux que je fasse ?

\#

> Ramasse les vêtements.

\#

> Tout de suite.

\#

> Peux-tu m'aider ?

\#

LESSON 4

Smart Grammar

The verb *pouvoir* (can, to be able)

The verb *pouvoir* is irregular. The chart shows its conjugation in the present tense.

je	peux	I can
tu	peux	you can
il/elle	peut	he/she can
nous	pouvons	we can
vous	pouvez	you can
ils/elles	peuvent	they can

Activity A

What can each of these people do? Write the correct form of the verb *pouvoir* in the blanks.

1 Elle _____ écrire.

2 Il _____ chanter.

3 Ils _____ nettoyer.

4 Elle _____ peindre.

Commands

French commands are verb forms used to give an order. Remember to drop the pronoun when you use a command becuase the conjugated verb already indicates to whom the command is directed. Look at the command forms below:

aider

(tu)	Aides !	Help!
(vous)	Aidez !	Help!
(nous)	Aidons !	Let's help!

ramasser

(tu)	Ramasses !	Pick up!
(vous)	Ramassez !	Pick up!
(nous)	Ramassons !	Let's pick up!

Activity B

Brigitte needs to get things done around the house. She asks her children to help out. Use the given verb and noun to write each command.

_____
ramasser/les vêtements

_____
peindre/la chambre

_____
organiser/le placard

_____
nettoyer/le sol

Où est-ce que tu es allé ?

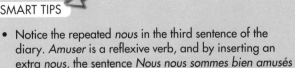
Diary Entry

Read Chantal's diary entry about where she went this week.

> *le 10 mai*
>
> *J'ai passé une bonne semaine. Avant-hier, mes amis et moi sommes allés à un concert de rock. Nous nous sommes bien amusés. Hier, ma mère et moi sommes allées dans un magasin pour acheter des vêtements. Ensuite, je suis allée en boîte avec mon copain et nous avons dansé toute la nuit. J'espère que nous retournerons danser très bientôt !*

s'amuser	to have fun
toute la nuit	all night
ensuite	afterwards

Activity A

Circle the correct answer for each question.

1 What did Chantal do the day before yesterday?
   a went to a concert   **b went to a club**

2 What did Chantal do yesterday?
   a went to a concert   **b went to a store**

3 What did Chantal do last night?
   a went to a club   **b went to a concert**

4 What does Chantal want to do again?
   a buy clothes   **b dance**

Activity B

Answer the following questions in French with a word or phrase from the diary entry.

1 How has Chantal's week been?

   _____

2 How was the concert the other day?

   _____

3 What did Chantal do after shopping?

   _____

4 Who did she go with?

   _____

Activity C

Write the sentence from the diary entry that tells what Chantal did each day.

1 avant-hier

   _____

2 hier

   _____

3 hier soir

   _____

LESSON 6

Words to Know

Core Words

aujourd'hui	today
avant-hier	day before yesterday
hier	yesterday
hier soir	last night
la semaine dernière	last week
le bar	bar
le cinéma	movie theater
le concert	concert
danser	to dance
le film	movie
le théâtre	theater

Activity A

Where did the following people go last night? Look at the pictures and write the French word for the place where each person went.

1 _____   2 _____

3 _____   4 _____

Activity B

Aujourd'hui, c'est mercredi. Write *hier soir, hier, avant-hier* or *la semaine dernière* to tell when you did each activity.

1 Mardi, j'ai dansé. _____

2 Lundi, j'ai vu un film. _____

3 Mercredi dernier, je suis allé/allée à un concert.

_____

4 Mardi soir, je suis allé/allée dans un bar. _____

Activity C

Complete the crossword puzzle in French using the English clue words.

ACROSS
2 yesterday
3 last week

DOWN
1 today
2 last night
4 day before yesterday

> **SMART TIP**
>
>
>
> When referring to a particular movie, use *le film*. Say *Je veux voir le film* (I want to see the movie). However, if you want to go to the movies, use *le ciné* or *le cinéma* and say *Je veux aller au ciné/cinéma.*

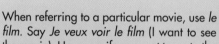

LESSON 7
Smart Phrases

Core Phrases

Qu'est-ce que tu as fait hier soir/hier/ avant-hier/ la semaine dernière ?
What did you do last night/ yesterday/the day before yesterday/last week?

Qu'est-ce que tu veux faire ?
What do you want to do?

Je veux rester à la maison.
I want to stay in.

Je veux sortir.
I want to go out.

Extra Phrases

Sortons.
Let's go out.

Allons prendre un pot.
Let's have a drink.

Activity A

What do you say if you want to...

1 ...ask what someone did last week?
_____

2 ...ask what someone wants to do?
_____

3 ...say you want to go out?
_____

4 ...say you want to stay in?
_____

CULTURE TIP

Paris is known for its nightlife. People might go out to dinner as late as 8 PM and stay out all night long. Often, clubs don't open until midnight and stay open until dawn.

Activity B

Édouard wants to take Manon out tonight. Manon doesn't want to go out. Édouard suggests activities, but to no avail. Put their dialogue in order to figure out what Édouard decides to do. (Notice Édouard uses the informal because Manon is his friend.)

___ **Édouard** Mais moi, je ne veux pas rester à la maison. Veux-tu aller danser ?

___ **Manon** Nous sommes allés au cinéma hier soir.

_1_ **Édouard** Qu'est-ce que tu veux faire ce soir ?

___ **Édouard** Veux-tu aller au cinéma ?

___ **Manon** Je veux rester à la maison ce soir.

___ **Édouard** Nous restons donc à la maison ce soir.

___ **Manon** Je suis allée danser avec mes amies hier.

Write in French what Édouard decides to do.

_____
_____
_____
_____
_____
_____

Your Turn

Qu'est-ce que tu veux faire ce soir ?

_____
_____
_____
_____

Smart Grammar

Past tense of *aller* with *être*

The verb *aller* is irregular in the past tense. It takes *être* as its helping verb and must agree in gender and number.

je	suis allé/allée	I went (m/f)
tu	es allé/allée	you went (m/f)
il/elle	est allé/allée	he/she went (m/f)
nous	sommes allés/allées	we went (m/f)
vous	êtes allés/allées	you went (m/f)
ils/elles	sont allés/allées	they went (m/f)

Examples

Elle est allée au magasin hier.   She went to the store yesterday.

Il est allé à la maison ce matin.   He went to the house this morning.

Activity A

Circle the word that best completes each sentence.

1   Il est _____ au concert hier.

   a allé   **b allées**

2   Je _____ allée chez le dentiste.

   a sont   **b suis**

3   Nous _____ allées au match du foot.

   a avons   **b sommes**

4   Ils sont _____ au cinéma.

   a allées   **b allés**

Activity B

Write the correct past tense form of *aller* in the blanks.

1   Je _____ chez ma mère hier soir.

2   Tu _____ travailler hier.

3   Il _____ à l'école ce matin.

4   Nous _____ au concert avant-hier.

5   Ils _____ au cinéma lundi dernier.

6   Mes amis _____ à Bruxelles l'année dernière.

Activity C

Now see if you can translate the sentences in Activity B. Write the English version of the sentences on the lines provided.

1   _____

2   _____

3   _____

4   _____

5   _____

6   _____

Your Turn

Answer the following questions in French.

1   Qu'est-ce que tu as fait hier soir ?

   _____

   _____

2   Qu'est-ce que tu as fait avant-hier ?

   _____

   _____

Activity A

Solve the following anagrams. Use the pictures as clues.

1 o i l t e t t e _ _ _ _ _ _ _ _

2 m l f i _ _ _ _

3 s r d a n e _ _ _ _ _ _

4 d r i p e n e _ _ _ _ _ _ _

5 u s i c n e i _ _ _ _ _ _ _

Activity B

Circle the sentence that best fits within the dialogue.

1 **Bruno** Qu'est-ce que tu veux faire ce soir ?

Agnès Je suis fatiguée.
a **J'ai écouté de la musique hier.**
b **Je veux rester à la maison ce soir.**

2 **Bruno** Non, je veux danser ! Sortons.

Agnès Non, Bruno.
a **J'ai dansé avec mes amies hier soir.**
b **Nous sommes allées au cinéma hier.**

3 **Bruno** Veux-tu aller prendre un pot dans un bar ?

Agnès Non.
a **J'ai déjà mangé ce soir.**
b **J'ai déjà bu du vin ce soir.**

4 **Bruno** Et le cinéma ? Allons voir un film !

Agnès Non.
a **Je veux rester à la maison.**
b **Qu'est-ce que tu as fait hier soir ?**

Activity C

Conjugate the following sentences in the past tense. Remember to include *être* as the helping verb.

1 Vous allez à l'ecole.

_____

2 Où est-ce que tu vas ?

_____

3 Nous allons à la bibliothèque.

_____

4 Je vais au restaurant.

_____

Activity D

Use the imperative forms of *aider* and *ramasser* to write the following commands.

1 help me clean (tu):

_____

2 help her (vous):

_____

3 pick up your clothes (tu):

_____

4 pick up that book (vous):

_____

Challenge

Change the commands in Activity D into questions using the verb *pouvoir*. For example, for the first question you would ask: *Peux-tu m'aider à ranger ?*

Internet Activity

Go to **www.berlitzbooks.com/5minute** for a list of forums where French learners can chat with native French speakers. Ask different people in the forum what they did *hier, hier soir, avant-hier* and *la semaine dernière*.

In this unit you will:
- **learn vocabulary for body and health.**
- **use adverbs of time.**
- **describe common symptoms and ailments.**
- **use the future tense with *aller* + infinitive verb.**

LESSON 1

Je suis malade

Dialogue

Odette asks her friend Robert to play tennis, but he's sick. They make an appointment for a different day. Listen to their conversation.

Robert Bonjour, Odette. Qu'est-ce que tu vas faire aujourd'hui ?

Odette Je vais jouer au tennis. Tu veux venir jouer avec moi ?

Robert Non, aujourd'hui je ne peux pas sortir parce que je suis malade.

Odette Quel dommage ! Si tu veux et si tu vas mieux, nous allons jouer jeudi ou vendredi.

Robert Oui, très bien. Si je vais mieux, nous allons jouer jeudi ou vendredi.

Odette D'accord. Appelle-moi jeudi et soigne-toi bien.

SMART TIP

Remember that Robert and Odette are friends, so they speak with each other informally using *tu* rather than *vous*.

Activity A

Choose the correct answer for each question.

1 When is Odette going to play tennis?

    a today   **b tomorrow**

2 Why doesn't Robert play with Odette?

    a He doesn't want to.   **b He can't.**

3 What other day might he play?

    a Monday   **b Friday**

4 Who is going to call on Thursday?

    a Odette   **b Robert**

Activity B

On Thursday, Robert sends Odette an *SMS* (text message). Read his message and Odette's response, then answer the questions.

1 Why can't Robert play on Thursday?

    a He's still sick.   **b He doesn't want to.**

2 What does Odette tell Robert?

    a not to call her   **b to feel better**

3 When will they talk again?

    a Sunday   **b Monday**

LESSON 2

Words to Know

Core Words

Les sports (Sports)

le baseball	baseball
le cyclisme	cycling
le football	soccer
la natation	swimming
le tennis	tennis

La santé (Health)

gras/grasse	fat (m/f)
malade	sick
mince	slender
peser	to weigh
le poids	weight
sain/saine	healthy (m/f)
le stress	stress
stressé/stressée	stressed (m/f)

Activity A

Write the name of the sport under each picture.

1 _____

3 _____

2 _____

4 _____

Activity B

Fill in the blanks with the correct French word.

1 Quel est votre _____ ?

weight

2 Il ne veut pas être _____.

fat

3 Elle mange bien pour rester _____

slender

   et _____.

healthy

4 Pourquoi êtes-vous _____ ?

stressed

5 Es-tu _____ Robert ?

sick

Activity C

Match the English word to the correct French translation.

1 slender
   - **a le stress**
   - **b mince**

2 soccer
   - **a le football**
   - **b le baseball**

3 to weigh
   - **a peser**
   - **b le poids**

4 healthy
   - **a malade**
   - **b sain**

> ### SMART TIP
>
> *Gymnastique* looks like the word *gymnase* (gym) but refers to the sport gymnastics. Examples: *Je vais au gymnase* (I'm going to the gym). *Anaïs fait de la gymnastique* (Anaïs does gymnastics).

LESSON 3

Smart Phrases

Core Phrases

Je suis malade.	I'm sick.
Je suis en bonne santé.	I'm healthy.
Je veux être en forme.	I want to be in shape.
Je veux perdre du poids.	I want to lose weight.
Je veux prendre du poids.	I want to gain weight.

Extra Phrases

Je crois que oui.	I think so.
Je suis désolé/désolée.	I'm sorry. (m/f)
Quel dommage !	What a shame!
Soigne-toi bien.	Feel better.

Activity A

What do you say if you want to…

1   …say you're healthy?

_____

2   …say you want to be in shape?

_____

3   …say you're sick?

_____

4   …say you want to lose weight?

_____

Activity B

Chose the best phrase for each picture.

1
    a Je suis malade.

    b Je suis en bonne santé.

2
    a Je veux être en forme.

    b Je suis malade.

3
    a Je veux perdre du poids.

    b Je suis en bonne santé.

4
    a Je veux perdre du poids.

    b Je veux prendre du poids.

5
    a Je suis en bonne santé.

    b Je veux prendre du poids.

SMART TIP

The term *santé* differs from *sain/saine* in that it is the noun for "health." The phrase *Je suis en bonne santé* literally translates as "I'm in good health."

LESSON 4
Smart Grammar

The future tense using *aller*

In Unit 9 you learned to use the future tense. You can also talk about the future using *aller* + infinitive verb.

Examples

Je vais jouer au tennis.	I'm going to play tennis.
Tu vas voir le dentiste.	You're going to see the dentist.
Nous allons habiter au Sénégal.	We're going to live in Senegal.
Ils vont parler au professeur.	They're going to talk to the teacher.

Activity A

Write what each person is going to do. The personal pronoun and verb are provided for you.

1   il, écrire _____

2   je, danser _____

3   elles, étudier _____

4   nous, jouer _____

5   tu, manger _____

6   elle, courir _____

SMART TIP

The future tense with *aller* is often used to talk about a plan. This form is more common than the simple future. For example, you will hear *Je vais jouer au tennis la semaine prochaine* (I am going to play tennis next week) instead of *Je jouerai au tennis la semaine prochaine* (I will play tennis next week).

Activity B

Make each sentence a question. The first one is done for you.

1   Tu vas regarder le film vendredi.
    <u>Quand est-ce que tu vas regarder le film ?</u>

2   Elle va me téléphoner demain.
    _____

3   Nous allons habiter à Bruges.
    _____

4   Fabien va te téléphoner.
    _____

5   Émille et Arnaud vont boire de la bière.
    _____

6   Vous allez manger du coq au vin.
    _____

Your Turn

Look at each picture and tell what is going to happen.

1   _____
    _____
    _____

2   _____
    _____
    _____

3   _____
    _____
    _____

4   _____
    _____
    _____

La médecine

Medical Advertisement

Read the advertisement. Remember to look for cognates and root words you know for help.

Le médicament contre le rhume

Il combat la fièvre et la toux.

Il atténue le mal de tête et de gorge.

Grâce à ce médicament, vous vous sentirez tout de suite mieux.

Vous n'avez pas besoin d'aller chez le médecin !

Vous n'avez pas besoin d'ordonnance !

Vous pouvez prendre ce médicament tous les jours.

atténuer	to ease
le rhume	cold (illness)
ordonnance	prescription

Activity A

Choose the correct answer for each question.

1 What is this ad for?

   a cold medicine　　**b pain medicine**

2 What does the medicine help with?

   a fever　　**b broken foot**

3 What does the medicine alleviate?

   a toothaches　　**b headaches**

4 Why don't you need to see a doctor to get this medicine?

   a You don't need a　　**b You don't need a**
   prescription.　　　　**shot.**

5 How often do you have to take this medicine?

   a once a month　　**b every day**

Médicament contre la toux

Soigne le mal de gorge.

Atténue la fièvre et la migraine.

À prendre deux fois par semaine.

Pour tout de suite se sentir mieux !

Ce médicament est uniquement délivré sur ordonnance.

Activity B

Choose the correct answer for each question.

1 What is this ad for?

   a stomach medicine　　**b cough medicine**

2 What does the medicine help with?

   a headaches　　　　**b sore throat**

3 What does the medicine alleviate?

   a fever　　　　**b toothache**

4 How often should you take this medicine?

   a every day　　　　**b twice a week**

5 Do you need to see a doctor to get this medicine?

   a yes　　　　**b no**

Activity C

Complete the following sentences to compare both medicines.

Les deux médicaments soignent _____.

Le médicament contre la toux soigne _____ et la contre le rhume soigne _____.

CULTURE TIP

When looking for a pharmacy in France, look for the lit up green and blue cross indicating an open pharmacy. Pharmacists in France are expected to give *conseils pharmaceutiques* (pharmaceutical advice) as a part of their job and are there to help you. If you have any questions before going to a doctor, you can head to a pharmacist for medical advice.

LESSON 6

Words to Know

Core Words

la fièvre	fever
le mal de gorge	sore throat
le mal de tête	headache
le mal au ventre	stomachache
la rage de dent	toothache
le rhume	cold
la toux	cough
le dentiste/la dentiste	dentist (m/f)
l'hôpital	hospital (m)
l'injection	shot (f)
le médecin	doctor
le médicament	medicine
l'ordonnance	prescription (f)

Activity A

You have various ailments. Circle the word that best completes the sentence.

1 J'ai une toux. J'ai besoin d'un _____.

   a dentiste   **b médecin**

2 J'ai mal aux dents. Je vais _____.

   a à l'hospital   **b chez le dentiste**

3 J'ai de la fièvre. Le médecin va vous donner
   une _____ pour acheter des médicaments.

   a injection   **b ordonnance**

4 J'ai mal à la tête. J'ai besoin de/d'_____.

   a médicament   **b une injection**

5 J'ai un rhume. Je vais _____.

   a chez le médecin   **b chez le dentiste**

Activity B

The following people are not feeling well. Look at the pictures and write the corresponding ailments.

 1 _____

 2 _____

 3 _____

 4 _____

Your Turn

Vous êtes médecin. Talk to your patient. *Qu'est-ce qu'il a ?
Il a besoin de quoi ?*

_____

_____

_____

_____

_____

SMART TIP

When you say you have an ailment, you literally
say that you have pain somewhere. Examples:

J'ai mal à la tête.	I have a headache.
J'ai mal au ventre.	I have a stomachache.
J'ai mal aux dents.	I have a toothache.

LESSON 7

Smart Phrases

Core Phrases

Où est-ce que ça fait mal ?	Where does it hurt?
J'ai mal au bras.	My arm hurts.
J'ai mal au dos.	My back hurts.
J'ai mal à la main.	My hand hurts.
J'ai mal au pied.	My foot hurts.
J'ai mal à la jambe.	My leg hurts.

Extra Phrases

Pouvez-vous me recommander un médecin/dentiste ?	Can you recommend a doctor/dentist?
Vous devez voir un médecin/dentiste.	You need to see a doctor/dentist.

Activity A

You are waiting to see the doctor. Tell the *infirmier/infirmière* (nurse, m/f) how you feel. Then tell him/her your symptoms.

Choose words or phrases from the box to write your description.

> le mal de tête   bras   J'ai mal au ventre.
> le mal de gorge   fièvre   J'ai mal au bras.

_____

_____

_____

_____

_____

Activity B

Write *le rapport d'infirmier/infirmière* (the nurse's report) based on what you told him/her in Activity A.

_____

_____

_____

Activity C

Look at the pictures and complete each sentence.

1 Elle a mal à la _____.

2 Elle a mal au _____.

3 Elle a mal au _____.

4 Il a mal au _____.

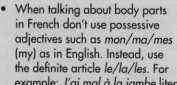

SMART TIPS

- When talking about body parts in French don't use possessive adjectives such as *mon/ma/mes* (my) as in English. Instead, use the definite article *le/la/les*. For example: *J'ai mal à la jambe* literally means "I have pain in the leg," but actually means "My leg hurts."

- The verb *devoir* is used to express obligation or necessity. It's an irregular –*ir* verb and is often translated as "should," "must," "ought to" or "need to." For example: *Vous devez voir un dentiste* (You need to see a dentist).

Smart Grammar

Adverbs of Time

Use the following words when talking about how frequently something happens.

souvent	often
parfois	sometimes
jamais	never
toujours	always
une fois/deux fois	once/twice
d'habitude	usually
tous les jours	every day

Examples

Je joue souvent au baseball.	I play baseball often.
D'habitude, Robert est en forme.	Robert is usually in shape.
Je ne fais jamais de gymnastique.	I never do gymnastics.
Je cours tous les jours.	I run every day.

Activity A

Choose the word that best describes how often you do these activities or how often this happens to you.

1   Je suis malade.
   a toujours   **b parfois**   **c jamais**

2   Je joue au football.
   a toujours   **b parfois**   **c jamais**

3   Je joue au tennis deux fois par semaine.
   a toujours   **b parfois**   **c jamais**

4   Je vais au gymnase.
   a toujours   **b parfois**   **c jamais**

Activity B

Translate these sentences from English to French.

1   I'm sometimes sick.

_____

2   I always go to the gym.

_____

3   I'm usually healthy.

_____

4   I play tennis once a week.

_____

5   I never take medicine.

_____

Activity C

Now translate these questions.

1   Do you always go to the gym on Tuesdays?

_____

2   Does Françoise play soccer every week?

_____

Your Turn

In French, tell what you do or don't do in these time frames.

1   tous les jours _____

2   souvent _____

3   jamais _____

4   d'habitude _____

SMART TIP

Remember that when you use *jamais*, you put the sentence in the negative form. Examples: *Je ne vais jamais chez le médecin* (I never go to the doctor), *Je ne prends jamais ce médicament* (I never take this medicine).

Activity A

Les frères Arnaud and Georges don't agree on anything. Arnaud will say something and Georges will immediately say the opposite or something else. Fill in Georges' half of the dialogue with the appropriate French phrase.

Arnaud Je suis malade.

Georges _____
I'm healthy.

Arnaud Je vais aller chez le dentiste.

Georges _____
I'm not going to see the dentist.

Arnaud J'ai mal au ventre.

Georges _____
I don't have a stomachache.

Arnaud Je ne veux pas aller chez le médecin.

Georges _____
I want to go to the doctor.

Arnaud Je cours parce que je veux perdre du poids.

Georges _____
I exercice becuase I want to gain weight.

Activity B

What's wrong with these sentences? Rewrite them so that they are grammatically correct.

1 J'ai mal au tête.

   _____

2 Je va habiter en France.

   _____

3 Je court deux fois par semaine.

   _____

4 Thierry allez courir au parc.

   _____

5 Nous allons mange les sandwiches.

   _____

6 J'ai mal à la pied.

   _____

Activity C

Use the pictures as clues to unscramble the anagrams. You will create words you learned in this unit.

1 y i l c c e s m _ _ _ _ _ _ _

2 s e n t i n _ _ _ _ _ _

3 ê e t a t m l e d _ _ _ _ _ _ _ _

4 n e d c a é m t i m _ _ _ _ _ _ _ _

5 è r e f v i _ _ _ _ _ _

6 e s t i t e n d _ _ _ _ _ _ _

> ## Challenge
>
> Answer the following questions based on your life.
>
> Qu'est-ce que vous allez manger demain pour le dîner ?
>
> _____
>
> Quel sport pratiquez-vous d'habitude ?
>
> _____
>
> Qu'allez-vous faire la semaine prochaine ?
>
> _____

Internet Activity

Go to **www.berlitzbooks.com/5minute** for a list of websites for French gyms. Find out what sports the gyms offer as well as the hours and costs. What sports would you sign up for?

A

l'adresse	lah·drehs	n address f
l'aéroport	lah·eh·roh·pohr	airport m
américain	ah·mehr·ee·kehN	American m
américaine	ah·mehr·ee·kehn	American f
anglais	ahn·gleh	English m
anglaise	ahn·glehz	English f
l'appartement	lah·pahr·tuh·mawN	apartment m
l'argent	lahr·zhawN	money m
l'arrêt d'autobus	lah·reh doh·toh·bews	bus stop m
l'assistant	lah·sees·tawN	assistant m
l'assistante	lah·sees·tawNt	assistant f
aujourd'hui	oh·zhoor·dwee	today
l'autobus	loh·toh·bews	n bus m
l'automne	lah·tohn	autumn m
avant-hier	ah·vawn·teeyehr	day before yesterday
l'avenue	lah·vuh·new	avenue f
l'avion	lah·veeyohN	plane m

B

le bagage	luh bah·gazh	luggage, baggage BE
le bar	luh bahr	bar
le baseball	luh bays·bohl	baseball
belge	behlzh	Belgian m/f
la Belgique	lah behl·zheek	Belgium
la bibliothèque	lah bee·blee·oh·tehk	library
la bière	lah beeyehr	beer
le billet	luh beeyeh	n ticket
blanc/blanche	blawN/blawNsh	white m/f
bleu/bleue	bluh	blue m/f
le blouson	luh bloo·sohN	jacket
boire	bwahr	v to drink
la boisson	lah bwahs·sohN	n drink
bon/bonne	bohN/bohn	good, warm
les bottes	lay boht	boots
le bureau	luh bew·roh	office

C

le café	luh kah·fay	coffee
le Canada	luh cah·nah·dah	Canada
canadien	cah·nah·dee·ehN	Canadian m
canadienne	cah·nah·dee·ehn	Canadian f
la carte bancaire	lah kahrt bawN·kayr	bank/debit card
la carte de crédit	lah kahrt duh kray·dee	credit card
la chambre	lah shawNbr	bedroom
le chapeau	luh shah·poh	hat
le chat	luh shah	cat
chaud	shoh	hot
la chemise	lah shuh·meez	shirt
le chemisier	luh shuh·mee·zeeyay	blouse
le chèque	luh shehk	n check
le chien	luh sheeyehN	dog
le cinéma	luh see·nay·mah	movie theater, cinema BE
le coin	luh kwehN	corner
le concert	luh kohN·sehr	concert
à côté de	ah koh·tay duh	next to
la couleur	lah koo·luhr	n color
le cousin	luh koo·zehN	cousin m
la cousine	lah koo·zeen	cousin f
la cravate	lah krah·vaht	n tie
la cuisine	la kwee·zeen	kitchen
le cyclisme	luh see·kleesm	cycling

D

danser	dawN·say	v dance
la dentiste	lah dawN·teest	dentist f
le dentiste	luh dawN·teest	dentist m
derrière	deh·reeyehr	behind
le dollar	luh dohl·lar	dollar
à droite	ah drwaht	to the right

adj adjective		BE British English	v verb	adv adverb	n noun

E

l'eau	loh	n water f
l'école	lay·kohl	school f
l'église	lay·glees	church f
l'employé	lahm·plwaheeyay	employee m
l'employée	lahm·plwaheeyay	employee f
les enfants	layz awN·fawN	children
Espagne	ehs·pah·nyuh	Spain
espagnol	ehs·pah·nyohl	Spanish/Spaniard m
espagnole	ehs·pah·nyohl	Spanish/Spaniard f
en espèces	awN ehs·pehs	in cash
les États-Unis	layz ay·tah·zew·nee	United States
l'été	lay·tay	summer
l'étudiant	lay·tew·dee·awN	student m
l'étudiante	ay·tew·dee·awNt	student f
extra large	ehks·trah lahrzh	extra large (clothing)

F

en face de	awn fahs duh	in front of
la famille	lah fah·meey	family
la femme	lah fahm	woman, wife
la fièvre	lah feeyehvr	fever, temperature BE
la fille	lah feey	girl, daughter
le film	luh feelm	movie, film BE
le fils	luh fees	son
le football	luh foot·bohl	soccer, football BE
français	frahN·say	French m
française	frahN·sehz	French f
la France	lah frahNs	France
le frère	luh frehr	brother
froid	frwah	adj cold (temperature)
le fromage	luh froh·mahzh	cheese
le fruit	luh frwee	fruit

G

les gants	lay gahN	gloves
le garçon	luh gahr·sohN	boy
la gare	lah gahr	train station
la gare routière	lah gahr roo·teeyehr	bus station
à gauche	ah gohsh	to the left
la glace	lah glahs	ice cream
grand/grande	grawN/grawNd	large m/f
la grand-mère	lah grahN·mehr	grandmother
le grand-père	luh grahN·pehr	grandfather
les grands-parents	lay grahN·pah·rawN	grandparents
gras/grasse	grah/grahs	adj fat m/f
le gymnase	luh zhihm·nahz	gym

H

une heure	ewn uhr	hour
à __ heures pile	ah __ uhr peel	at __ o'clock sharp
hier	eeyehr	yesterday
hier soir	eeyehr swahr	last night
l'hiver	lee·vehr	winter
l'homme	lohm	man m
l'hôpital	loh·pee·tahl	hospital m
humide	ew·meed	humid

I

l'immeuble	lee·muhbl	building m
l'injection	leen·zhek·seeyohN	injection, shot f

J

jaune	zhohn	yellow
le jour	luh zhoohr	day
le journal	luh zhoohr·nahl	newspaper
le/la journaliste	luh/lah zhoohr·nahl·eest	journalist m/f
la jupe	lah zhewp	skirt
le jus	luh zhew	juice

---

adj adjective   BE British English   v verb   adv adverb   n noun

L

le lait	luh lay	milk
les légumes	lay lay·gewm	vegetables
du liquide	dew lee·keed	n cash
loin de	lwehn duh	far from

M

le magasin	luh mah·gah·zehN	n store, shop
le magazine	luh mah·gah·zeen	magazine
la maison	lah may·zohN	n house
le mal de gorge	luh mahl duh gohrzh	sore throat
le mal de tête	luh mahl duh teht	headache
le mal au ventre	luh mahl oh vawNtr	stomach ache
malade	mah·lahd	sick, ill BE
manger	mahN·zhay	v to eat
le manteau	luh mawN·toh	coat
le mari	luh mah·ree	husband
marron	mah·rohN	brown
le médecin	luh mayd·sehN	doctor
le médicament	luh may·dee·kah·mawN	medicine
la mère	lah mehr	mother
mince	mehNs	slender
une minute	ewn mee·newt	n minute
moyen	mwoh·yehN	adj medium m
moyenne	mwoh·yehn	adj medium f

N

la natation	lah nah·tah·seeyohN	n swimming
la neige	lah nehzh	snow
le neveu	luh nuh·vuh	nephew
la nièce	lah neeyehs	niece
noir/noire	nwahr	black m/f
la nourriture	lah noo·ree·tewr	food
le nuage	luh newazh	cloud
le numéro	luh new·may·roh	number

O

les œufs	lay zuh	eggs
l'oiseau	lwah·zoh	bird m
l'oncle	lohNkl	uncle m
l'ordonnance	lohr·dohn·awNs	prescription f

P

le pain	luh pehN	bread
le pantalon	luh pawN·tah·lohN	pants, trousers BE
les pâtes	lay paht	pasta
les parents	lay pah·rawN	parents
le passeport	luh pahs·pohr	passport
le patron	luh pah·trohN	boss m
la patronne	lah pah·trohn	boss f
le père	luh pehr	father
peser	puh·say	v to weigh
petit/petite	puh·tee/puh·teet	small m/f
le petit-fils	luh puh·tee·fees	grandson
la petite-fille	lah puh·teet·feey	granddaughter
la pièce	lah peeyehs	room
le placard	luh plah·kahr	closet
la pluie	lah plwee	n rain
le poids	luh pwah	weight
le poisson	luh pwahs·sohN	fish
les pommes de terre	lay pohm duh tehr	potatoes f
la poste	lah pohst	post office
le poulet	luh poo·lay	chicken
prendre	prawNdr	v to take/eat/ drink
près de	preh duh	near
le printemps	luh prehN·tehm	spring
le professeur	luh proh·feh·suhr	teacher
la profession	lah proh·fehseeyohN	profession

---

adj adjective	BE British English	v verb	adv adverb	n noun

R

la rage de dent	lah rahzh duh dawN	toothache
le reçu	luh ruh·sew	receipt
le rhume	luh rhewm	n cold (sickness)
le riz	luh ree	rice
la robe	lah rohb	n dress
rose	rohz	pink
rouge	roozh	red
le Royaume-Uni	luh roy·ohm ew·nee	United Kingdom
la rue	lah rew	street

S

sain/saine	sehN/sehn	healthy m/f
la saison	lah say·zohN	n season
la salade	lah sah·lahd	salad
le salaire	luh sah·layr	salary
la salle	lah sahl	room
la salle à manger	ah mawN·zhay	dining room
la salle de bain	duh bahN	bathroom
la salle de classe	duh klahs	classroom
la salle de séjour	duh say·zhoor	living room
les sandales	lay sahN·dahl	sandals f
la santé	lah sahN·tay	health
une seconde	ewn suh·gohNd	n second
le/la secrétaire	luh/lah suh·kray·tayr	secretary m/f
la semaine	lah suh·mehn	week
la semaine dernière	lah suh·mehn dehr·neeyehr	last week
le Sénégal	luh say·nay·gahl	Senegal
la sœur	lah suhr	sister
le soleil	luh soh·lehy	sun
la soupe	lah soop	soup
les sports	lay spohr	sports m
la station de métro	la stah·seeyohN duh may·troh	subway, metro BE station

le stress	luh strehs	n stress
Suisse	swees	Switzerland
suisse	swees	Swiss
le supermarché	luh sew·pehr·mahr·shay	supermarket

T

la taille	lah tie	size
la tante	lah tahNt	aunt
la tarte	lah tahrt	cake
une taxe	ewn tahks	sales tax
le tee-shirt	luh tee·shuhrt	T-shirt
le téléphone	luh tay·lay·fohn	n telephone
le temps	luh tawN	weather
le tennis	luh teh·nees	tennis
le thé	luh tay	tea
le théâtre	luh tay·ahtr	theater
la toux	lah too	n cough
le travail	luh trah·vie	job
travailler	trah·vie·ay	v to work

V

les vacances	lay vah·kawNs	n vacation, holiday BE
la valise	lah vah·leez	suitcase
le vent	luh vawN	wind
vert/verte	vehr/vehrt	green m/f
les vêtements	lay veht·mawN	clothing m
la viande	lah veeyaNd	meat
violet/violette	veeyoh·lay/veeyoh·leht	purple m/f
la voiture	lah vwah·tewr	car
le vol	luh vohl	flight
le voyage	luh vwah·yahzh	n trip

---

adj adjective   BE British English   v verb   adv adverb   n noun

Numbers

zéro	zay·roh	0
un	uhN	1
deux	duh	2
trois	trwah	3
quatre	kahtr	4
cinq	sehNk	5
six	sees	6
sept	seht	7
huit	weet	8
neuf	nuhf	9
dix	dees	10
onze	ohNz	11
douze	dooz	12
treize	trehz	13
quatorze	kah·tohrz	14
quinze	kehNz	15
seize	sehz	16
dix-sept	deez·seht	17
dix-huit	deez·weet	18
dix-neuf	deez·nuhf	19
vingt	vehN	20
trente	trawNt	30
trente-et-un	trawNt·ay·uhN	31
trente-deux	trawNt·duh	32
trente-trois	trawNt·trwah	33
trente-quatre	trawNt·kahtr	34
trente-cinq	trawNt·sehNk	35
quarante	kah·rawNt	40
cinquante	sehn·kawNt	50
soixante	swah·sawNt	60

Days

lundi	luhN·dee	Monday
mardi	mahr·dee	Tuesday
mercredi	mehr·kruh·dee	Wednesday
jeudi	zhuh·dee	Thursday
vendredi	vawN·druh·dee	Friday
samedi	sahm·dee	Saturday
dimanche	dee·mahNsh	Sunday

Months

janvier	zhahN·veeyay	January
février	fehv·reeyay	February
mars	marhs	March
avril	ah·vreel	April
mai	may	May
juin	zhew·uhN	June
juillet	zhweeyay	July
août	ooht	August
septembre	sehp·tawmbr	September
octobre	ohk·tohbr	October
novembre	noh·vawmbr	November
décembre	day·sawmbr	December

adj   adjective   BE   British English   v   verb   adv   adverb   n   noun

Countries/Nationalities

Allemagne	ah·le·mawn·yuh	Germany
allemand	ah·le·mawN	German m
allemande	ah·le·mawnd	German f

Australie	oh·stray·lee	Australia
australien	oh·stray·lee·ehN	Australian m
australienne	oh·stray·lee·ehn	Australian f

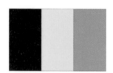

Belgique	behl·zheek	Belgium
belge	behlzh	Belgian m
belge	behlzh	Belgian f

Cameroun	cam·roohn	Cameroon
camerounais	cam·roohn·eh	Cameroonian m
camerounaise	cam·roohn·ehz	Cameroonian f

Canada	cah·nah·dah	Canada
canadien	cah·nah·dee·ehN	Canadian m
canadienne	cah·nah·dee·ehn	Canadian f

Espagne	ehs·pah·nyuh	Spain
espagnol	ehs·pah·nyohl	Spanish m
espagnole	ehs·pah·nyohl	Spanish f

Etats-Unis	ay·tah·zew·nee	United States
américain	ah·mehr·ee·kehN	American m
américaine	ah·mehr·ee·kehn	American f

France	frahNs	France
français	frahN·say	French m
française	frahN·sehz	French f

adj adjective	BE British English	v verb	adv adverb	n noun

Countries/Nationalities

Haïti	i·ayh·tee	Haiti
haïtien	i·ay·tee·ehN	Haitian m
haïtienne	i·ay·tee·ehn	Haitian f

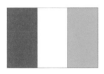

Irlande	eer·lahnd	Ireland
irlandais	eer·lahn·deh	Irish m
irlandaise	eer·lahn·dehz	Irish f

Italie	ee·tah·lee	Italy
italien	ee·tah·lee·ehN	Italian m
italienne	ee·tah·lee·ehn	Italian f

Portugal	por·too·gal	Portugal
portugais	por·too·geh	Portuguese m
portugaise	por·too·gehz	Portuguese f

Royaume-Uni	roy·ohm ew·nee	United Kingdom
anglais	ahn·gleh	English m
anglaise	ahn·glehz	English f

le Sénégal	luh say·nay·gahl	Senegal
sénégalais	say·nay·gahl·eh	Senegalese m
sénégalaise	say·nay·gahl·ehz	Senegalese f

Suisse	swees	Switzerland
suisse	swees	Swiss m
suisse	swees	Swiss f

adj   adjective   BE   British English   v   verb   adv   adverb   n   noun

Colors

Les couleurs   ley koo·luhr   colours BE

blanc/blanche
blawN/blawNsh
white m/f

rose
rohz
pink

bleu/bleue
bluh
blue m/f

rouge
roozh
red

jaune
zhohn
yellow

vert/verte
vehr/vehrt
green m/f

marron
mah·rohN
brown

violet/violette
veeyoh·lay/veeyoh·leht
purple m/f

noir/noire
nwahr
black m/f

Seasons

l'automne
lah·tohn
autumn

l'hiver
lee·vehr
winter

l'été
lay·tay
summer

le printemps
luh prehN·tehm
spring

adj   adjective   BE   British English   v   verb   adv   adverb   n   noun

Extra Words

les affaires	lays ah·fayhr	business
aîné	ay·nay	older m
aînée	ay·nay	older f
après-midi	ahprahy·meedee	afternoon
l'article	lahr·teek	article
beaucoup (de)	boh·koo duh	a lot (of)
le beau-fils	luh boh·fees	son-in-law
le beau-frère	luh boh·frehr	brother-in-law
le beau-père	luh boh·pehr	father-in-law
la belle-fille	lah behl·feey	daughter-in-law
la belle-mère	lah behl·mehr	mother-in-law
la belle-sœur	lah behl·suhr	sister-in-law
cadet	cah·day	younger m
cadette	cah·deht	younger f
les centimes	lay sahn·teem	cents
courir	koor·eer	to run
un demi	uhN deh·mee	half m
une demie	ewn deh·mee	half f
difficile	dee·fee·seehl	difficult
dur	dehr	hard
l'employeur	lehm·ploy·ehr	employer m
l'employeuse	lehm·ploy·ews	employer f
l'enterprise	lehn·tahyr·prees	company f
l'escale	lehscahl	stop/ layover f
les escaliers	lays ay·scahl·eeyah	stairs m
facile	fahseehl	easy
le fenêtre	luh fehn·eht	window
l'hôtel	lohtehl	hotel m
intéressant	ehn·tahyr·eh·sehN	interesting
intéressante	ehn·tahyr·eh·sehnt	interesting
le jardin	luh zhahr·dehn	garden
jouer	zhew·ay	to play
matin	mah·tehn	morning
la monnaie	lah moh·nay	change
nager	nazh·ay	to swim
la pièce	lah peeyehs	coin
le portefeuille	luh pohrt·foyuh	wallet
porter	pohr·tay	to wear
un quart	uhN kahr	quarter
la réservation	lah rhes·ehr·vah·see·ohN	reservation
soir	swahr	night
le sol	luh sohwl	sun
voyager	vwoyh·ah·zhay	to travel

adj	adjective	BE	British English	v	verb	adv	adverb	n	noun

Unit 1 Lesson 1

Activity A

1 T; 2 T; 3 F; 4 T

Activity B

Je m'appelle Martine. **Comment vous appelez-vous ?;** Je m'appelle Pierre. **Enchanté.;** Je suis française. Et vous, **d'où venez-vous ?;** Je suis **belge.**

Lesson 2

Activity A

1 Bonjour !; 2 Comment vous appelez-vous ?;
3 D'où venez-vous ?; 4 Au revoir !

Activity B

1 Bonsoir.; 2 Bonne nuit.; 3 Bonjour.

Lesson 3

Activity A

l'Amerique du Nord: 3
l'Europe, top to bottom: 5; 4; 1
l'Afrique: 2

Activity B

From left to right: 3; 1; 4; 2

Lesson 4

Activity A

1 je; 2 elle; 3 il; 4 tu

Activity B

1 elles; 2 ils; 3 nous; 4 nous

Activity C

1 je; 2 elle; 3 il; 4 elles; 5 ils

Lesson 5

Activity A

langue; nationalité; français; anglais

Activity B

1 canadien/canadienne; 2 belge; 3 français; 4 pays

Lesson 6

Activity A

1 française; 2 américaine; 3 anglais; 4 australien

Activity B

1 espagnole; 2 anglaise; 3 française; 4 américaine;
5 canadienne

Lesson 7

Activity A

1 Vous êtes français/française ?; 2 Je parle bien.;
3 Je parle un peu.

Your Turn

Answers may vary. Possible answers:
Q1 Bonjour ! Vous êtes français?   A1 Oui, je suis français.
Q2. Parlez-vous français?   A2 Oui, je parle bien.

Lesson 8

Activity A

1 suis; 2 es; 3 Es; 4 est

Activity B

1 êtes; 2 sommes; 3 sont; 4 sont

Your Turn

êtes; suis; êtes; suis; est

Review

Activity A

Nom	Pays	Nationalité
Madeline	la France	française
Paul	la Belgique	belge
Claire	le Canada	canadienne
Brian	les États-Unis	américain
Katie	le Royaume-Uni	anglaise

Activity B

1 Tu es américain/américaine.; 2 Lisa est espagnole.; 3 Vous êtes canadien/canadienne.; 4 Emile est français.

Activity C

Guide	Bonjour ! Bienvenue en France !
Alex	Bonjour ! Je m'appelle Alex Cromwell. Et vous, comment vous appelez-vous ?
Guide	Je m'appelle Marc. Enchanté.
Alex	Enchanté. Vous êtes français ?
Guide	Oui. D'où venez-vous ?
Alex	Je viens des États-Unis. Parlez-vous anglais ?
Guide	Un peu.
Alex	Je parle anglais et français.
Guide	Bien!
Alex	Au revoir, Marc.
Guide	Au revoir !

Activity D

L	E	D	É	T	A	T	S	U	N	I	S	S	S	O	S
É	Y	P	I	O	S	E	É	N	Ç	N	A	I	É	L	B
N	A	A	T	L	C	S	N	A	N	A	D	A	N	A	C
A	D	A	N	N	C	A	É	U	D	P	O	L	É	A	B
C	A	N	A	D	I	E	N	N	E	P	C	G	G	E	E
Á	U	R	A	N	A	D	É	E	N	S	E	N	A	H	L
E	F	R	A	N	Ç	A	I	S	G	N	W	A	L	U	G
B	E	L	G	I	Q	U	E	N	E	Q	O	S	Á	D	E

Challenge

Belgique; Belge

Activity E

1 Bonjour ! Je m'appelle Laure.; 2 Nous sommes du Canada.; 3 Corinne est de la Belgique. Corinne est belge.; 4 Marc est américain.; 5 Je parle français.; 6 Annie est canadienne.

Unit 2 Lesson 1

Activity A

1 T; 2 F; 3 T; 4 T

Activity B

1 personnes: garçons; filles; hommes; femmes.; 2 choses: maisons; immeubles; voitures; autobus.; 3 animaux: chats; chiens

Lesson 2

Activity A

1 a. oiseau; b. femme; c. homme; d. garçon. 2 a. homme; b. autobus; c. chien; d. garçon; e. immeuble; f. chat; g. femme; h. voiture

Activity B

1 masculin; 2 masculin; 3 féminin; 4 féminin; 5 masculin; 6 féminin; 7 masculin; 8 masculin

Lesson 3

Activity A

1 Regarde les gens !; 2 Regarde les animaux !

Activity B

Answers may vary. Possible answers:
Chère Elaine,
Je m'amuse bien ici, et j'apprends (un peu) de français. Regarde les personnes ! Regarde les maisons ! Regarde le chien ! Regarde les animaux ! Tu me manques.

Lesson 4

Activity A

1 hommes; 2 sacs; 3 crayons; 4 oiseaux

Activity B

1 le; 2 la; 3 les; 4 les; 5 la; 6 l'

Activity C

1 le chat; 2 les femmes; 3 les voitures; 4 la maison

Your Turn

1 la; 2 les; 3 le; 4 le; 5 la

Lesson 5

Activity A

1 c; 2 b; 3 d; 4 a

Activity B

Rue: rue Servan; Numéro: 10. Ville: Lyon; Pays: France

Lesson 6

Activity A

dix-neuf
vingt-quatre, vingt-cinq, vingt-six, vingt-sept, vingt-huit, vingt-neuf

Activity B

1	un	4	quatre
6	six	9	neuf
13	treize	12	douze
18	dix-huit	15	quinze
10	dix	22	vingt-deux
30	trente	14	quatorze

Activity C

1 14th Street; 2 26 Victor Hugo Avenue; 3 Téléphone: (178) 375-4219; 4 Zip Code: 38001

Lesson 7

Activity A

Answers may vary. Possible answers:
Je m'appelle _____.; Mon adresse est _____.; Ma date de naissance est _____; Mon numéro de téléphone est le _____.

Activity B

1 a; 2 b; 3 a; 4 b

Lesson 8

Activity A

je parle; tu parles; il/elle parle; nous parlons; vous parlez; ils/elles parlent

Activity B

je finis; tu finis; il/elle finit; nous finissons; vous finissez; ils/elles finissent

Activity C

Nick habite à dix Rue Orchard; Julia et Max habitent à vingt-quatre Rue Sept; Amy et moi habitons à seize Rue Main.

Your Turn

J'enseigne anglais et français.; Amandine enseigne anglais.

Review

Activity A

1 trois garçons; 2 une maison; 3 deux téléphones; 4 cinq femmes

Activity B

1 Thierry habite à vingt-cinq Rue de Rivoli; 2 Le numéro de téléphone de Thierry est zéro cinq, zéro six, quatre cinq, cinq six, six six.; 3 Corrine et Mark habitent à trente Avenue Baudin; 4 Le numéro de téléphone de Christine est zéro quatre, trois trois, cinq deux, sept cinq, un neuf; 5 David habite à quinze Rue Perronet.

Challenge

Answers may vary. Possible answers: Il habite à Rue Washington.; Elle habite à Avenue Myrtle.; Il est Américain.; Elle parle espagnol.

Activity C

1 les; 2 les; 3 le; 4 la

Activity D

Astrid Bonjour ! Comment vous appelez-vous ?
Vous Bonjour ! Je m'appelle (your name).
Astrid Bien. Quel est votre numéro de téléphone ?
Vous Mon numéro de téléphone est (your phone number).
Astrid Quelle est votre adresse ?
Vous Mon adresse est (your address).
Astrid Et le code postal ?
Vous Mon code postal est (your zip code).
Astrid Pour finir, quelle est votre date de naissance ?
Vous Mon date de naissance est (your date of birth).
Astrid Excellent ! Bienvenue à l'Institut de langues de Marseille !
Vous Merci.

Unit 3 Lesson 1

Activity A

1 dix-huit heures; 2 oui; 3 cinquante-cinq minutes; 4 Lyon

Activity B

1 Quelle heure est-il ?; 2 Il est dix-huit heures.; 3 Il est tôt ! Combien de temps reste-t-il avant la fin du match ?; 4 Il reste cinquante-cinq minutes.

Lesson 2

Activity A

1 Il est seize heures moins le quart.; 2 Il est treize heures et quart.; 3 Il est vingt heures et demie.; 4 Il est minuit.

Activity B

1 Il est tôt !; 2 Il est tard !; 3 Il est tôt !; 4 Il est tard !

Activity C

1 Quelle heure est-il ?; 2 Il est tôt !; 3 Il est tard !; 4 Il est deux heures.

Lesson 3

Activity A

1 quarante-quatre; 2 trente-deux; 3 soixante-sept; 4 cinquante-huit

Activity B

1 Il reste quinze minutes.; 2 Il reste six heures et vingt-huit minutes.; 3 Il reste une heure et quarante-cinq minutes.; 4 Il reste une minute.

Your Turn

Il est seize heures et douze minutes. Il reste trente-trois minutes.; Il est seize heures et vingt-deux minutes. Il reste vingt-trois minutes.; Il est seize heures et trente-deux minutes. Il reste treize minutes.; Il est seize heures et quarante-deux minutes. Il reste trois minutes.

Lesson 4

Activity A

je réponds
tu réponds
il/elle répond
nous répondons
vous répondez
ils/elles répondent

Activity B

1 Je vends. 2 Nous répondons. 3 Elle descend. 4 Elles attendent.

Your Turn

Answers will vary. Possible answers:
La femme attend.
La fille descend les escaliers.

Lesson 5

Activity A

1 a; 2 a; 3 a; 4 a

Activity B

1 faire ses devoirs; 2 appeler Maud; 3 faire la lessive; 4 aller chez le médecin

Lesson 6

Activity A

1 dimanche; 2 lundi et jeudi ; 3 vendredi; 4 mardi; 5 mercredi et samedi

Activity B

1 lundi, le 17 novembre; 2 samedi, le 5 juin; 3 mercredi, le 21 septembre; 4 vendredi, le 8 avril; 5 mardi, le 31 janvier; 6 dimanche, le 12 août; 7 jeudi, le 25 mars; 8 dimanche, le 14 octobre; 9 lundi, le 29 mai; 10 mardi, le 2 décembre; 11 vendredi, le 15 juillet; 12 mercredi, le 18 février

Lesson 7

Activity A

1 b; 2 b; 3 a; 4 b

Activity B

1 Quel jour sommes-nous ?; 2 Quelle est la date aujourd'hui ?; 3 Quel mois sommes-nous ?; 4 Quelle année sommes-nous ?

Lesson 8

Activity A

1 fais; 2 fait; 3 font; 4 faisons

Activity B

1 c; 2 a; 3 b; 4 d

Your Turn

Answers will vary. Possible answers:
Je fais des achats le samedi.
Je fais du football le dimanche.

Review

Activity A

The order of the activities may vary. Possible order:
2 Amélie appelle Alain à vingt et un heures moins le quart.; 3 Amélie fait la cuisine à dix-huit heures.; 4 Amélie fait la lessive à huit heures moins le quart.; 4 Amélie fait ses devoirs à onze heures et le quart.

Activity B

1 Il reste deux heures, trente-quatre minutes et treize secondes.; 2 Il reste une heure et dix minutes.; 3 Il reste douze minutes et trente-neuf secondes.; 4 Il reste une heure, vingt-sept minutes et vingt-cinq secondes.

Activity C

1 dimanche, le vingt et un mars 2009; 2 samedi, le treize mars 2009; 3 mardi, le vingt-trois mars 2009; 4 lundi, le quinze mars 2009

Unit 4 Lesson 1

Activity A

1 F; 2 F; 3 F; 4 T

Activity B

1 a; 2 a; 3 b; 4 b

Lesson 2

Activity A

Il y a cinq personnes dans ma **famille**. Thomas, c'est mon **père**. Ma **mère** s'appelle Hélène. Rachel, c'est ma **sœur**. Paul est le **mari** de Rachel.

Activity B

1 frère et sœur; 2 frère; 3 mère; 4 père; 5 parents; 6 fils; 7 fille; 8 enfants; 9 femme; 10 mari

Lesson 3

Activity A

1 Vous êtes combien dans ta famille ?; 2 Dans ma famille, nous sommes huit. Regarde la photo.; 3 Quelle grande famille !; 4 Oui, ma famille est grande. Est-ce que ta famille est grande ?; 5 Non. Ma famille est petite. Dans ma famille, nous sommes quatre.

Activity B

1 Quelle petite famille !; 2 Quelle grande famille !; 3 Quelle grande famille !; 4 Quelle petite famille !

Your Turn

Answers will vary. Possible answer:
Ma famille est petite. Dans mon famille, nous sommes trois.

Lesson 4

Activity A

1 ma; 2 ton; 3 Votre; 4 mes; 5 tes; 6 vos; 7 Notre; 8 nos

Activity B

1 e; 2 b; 3 h; 4 d; 5 c; 6 g; 7 a; 8 f

Lesson 5

Activity A

1 son oncle.; 2 sa mère.; 3 son frère.; 4 sa tante.

Activity B

1 cousin; 2 cousine; 3 grand-mère; 4 neveu

Lesson 6

Activity A

1 cousine; 2 neveu; 3 tante; 4 petit-fils; 5 grand-père; 6 grand-parents

Activity B

1 a; 2 a; 3 a; 4 a; 5 a; 6 b

Lesson 7

Activity A

1 d; 2 c; 3 b; 4 a

Activity B

1 Je t'aime.; 2 Je t'adore.; 3 J'ai une famille proche.; 4 Es-tu marié/mariée ?

Your Turn

Answers will vary. Possible answers:
Je suis mariée. Mes parents sont marié. Ma sœur est célibataire.

Lesson 8

Activity A

1 un grand-père; 2 des filles; 3 une femme; 4 des hommes

Activity B

Answers will vary. Possible answers: 1 Tu as un frère.; 2 J'ai un cousin.; 3 Elles ont deux tantes.; 4 Vous avez trois nièces.

Your Turn

Answers will vary. Possible answers: 1 Oui, j'ai deux tantes. / Non, je n'ai pas des tantes.; 2 Oui, j'ai un neveu. / Non, je n'ai pas des neveux.; 3 Oui, mes oncles ont quatre enfants. / Non, mes oncles n'ont pas des enfants.; 4 Oui, mes cousins ont deux enfants. / Non, mes cousins n'ont pas des enfants.

Review

Activity A

Monique	Voici mon **grand-père**, Alain. Et voilà ma grand-mère, Nathalie.
Antoine	Et qui est cette femme ?
Monique	C'est ma **cousine**, Michelle, et c'est son **frère**, Didier.
Antoine	Cette dame, c'est ta **mère** ?
Monique	Non, c'est ma **tante**, Carmen. C'est la **sœur** de ma mère. Michele et Didier sont ses **enfants**.
Antoine	Alors, ta mère, c'est cette dame ?
Monique	(laughs) Non, c'est ma **tante**, Lisette, la **femme** de mon **oncle** Maurice. C'est le **frère** de mon **père**.
Antoine	Ta **famille** est grande. Mais où est (where is) ta mère ?
Monique	Mes **parents** ne sont pas ici (are not here).

Activity B

1 Nathalie **est sa grand-mère.**; 2 Michele et Didier **sont ses cousins.**; 3 Carmen et Lisette **sont ses tantes.**; 4 Maurice **est son oncle.**

Activity C

Answers will vary. Possible answers:

Antoine	Ma famille est petite.
Antoine	Non, je n'ai pas des frères.
Antoine	Oui, j'ai deux oncles.

Activity D

Antoine	**Cet** homme, c'est votre neveu ?
Monique	Non, c'est le neveu de monsieur.
Antoine	Qui est **cette** femme ?
Monique	Cette femme, c'est ma nièce.
Antoine	**Ces** filles sont vos filles ?
Monique	Non, **ces** filles sont mes petites-filles.

Activity E

1 Ils ont deux enfants.; 2 Ils ont trois enfants.; 3 Elle a deux filles.; 4 Il a un fils.

Unit 5 Lesson 1

Activity A 1 T; 2 T; 3 F; 4 F

Activity B 1 a; 2 b; 3 b; 4 b

Lesson 2

Activity A 1 les fruits; 2 le café; 3 la soupe; 4 la bière

Activity B

Answers may vary. Possible answers: 1 Je mange du pain et boire du café.; 2 Je mange des fruits et boire de l'eau.; 3 Je mange de la soupe et boire de la bière.

Lesson 3

Activity A 1 J'ai faim.; 2 J'ai soif.; 3 J'ai faim.; 4 J'ai soif.

Activity B

1 J'ai envie de manger une salade.; 2 J'ai envie de boire une bière.

Activity C 1 Prenons le petit-déjeuner.; 2 Déjeunons.; 3 Dînons.

Lesson 4

Activity A

1 Où; 2 Quelle; 3 Qui; 4 Quand; 5 Qui; 6 Quelle; 7 quoi; 8 Quelle

Activity B

Answers will vary. Possible answers: 1 Quelle fille est ton sœur ?; 2 Quand est-ce que vous travaillez ?; 3 Qui est cet homme ?; 4 Où est ta maison ?

Activity C 1 Pourquoi; 2 Qui; 3 Quand; 4 Lequel/Laquelle; 5 Où

Your Turn

Answers may vary. Possible answers:
1 Comment t'appelle ta mère ? ; 2 Quelle heure est-il ?; 3 Qui sont ces hommes ?; 4 Où est-ce que vous habitez ?

Lesson 5

Activity A 1 b; 2 b; 3 a; 4 a

Activity B 1 Quelle entrée voulez-vous ?; 2 Comme entrée, je prends une salade.; 3 Et comme plat principal ?; 4 Je voudrais le poulet aux pommes de terre.

Lesson 6

Activity A 1 entrée; 2 plat principal;
3 dessert; 4 plat principal

Activity B 1 a; 2 b; 3 a

Your Turn Answers will vary.
Possible answers are:

Lesson 7

Activity A

1 Bon appétit.; 2 L'addition, s'il vous plaît.; 3 C'est délicieux !; 4 Puis-je voir la carte des vins (s'il vous plait) ?

Activity B 1 b; 2 a; 3 b; 4 a

Your Turn

Answers will vary.

Lesson 8

Activity A 1 veut; 2 voulons; 3 veulent; 4 Voulez

Activity B

1 Je veux le poulet pour l'entrée.; 2 Je ne veux pas le fromage pour l'entrée.; 3 Je veux le poisson pour le plat principal.; 4 Je ne veux pas la viande pour le plat principal.; 5 Je veux le gâteau pour le dessert.; 6 Je ne veux pas la glace pour le dessert.

Review

Activity A

Le déjeuner: 1 Je veux de la soupe et boire de l'eau.; 2 Tu veux de la soupe et boire de l'eau.; 3 Il/elle veut de la soupe et boire de l'eau.; 4 Nous voulons de la soupe et boire de l'eau.; 5 Vous voulez de la soupe et boire de l'eau.; 6 Ils/elles veulent de la soupe et boire de l'eau.
Le dîner: 1 J'aime bien du steak et boire de la bière.; 2 Tu aimes bien du steak et boire de la bière.; 3 Il/elle aime bien du steak et boire de la bière.; 4 Nous aimons bien du steak et boire de la bière.; 5 Vous aimez bien du steak et boire de la bière.; 6 Ils aiment bien du steak et boire de la bière.

Activity B

Activity C

Julien	J'ai faim.
Eve	Qu'est-ce que tu **veux** manger ?
Julien	Je **veux** de manger du poulet.
Eve	Allons au **restaurant**.
In the car	
Julien	Où est le restaurant ?
Eve	C'est par là. (Points to a restuarant down the block.)
At the restaurant before eating	
Eve	Qu'est-ce que tu **veux** pour le plat principal ?
Julien	Je **voudrais** le poulet.
At the restaurant after eating	
Eve	L'addition, s'il vous plaît.

Unit 6 Lesson 1

Activity A

1 c; 2 d; 3 b; 4 a

Activity B

(Crossword: 2-across **température**; 1-down **celsius** (c, l, s, i, u, s); 2-down **degrés** (d, e, g, r, é, s))

Lesson 2

Activity A

Quel temps fait-il à Haïti ?; Il fait chaud et il y a du soleil.; Quelle température fait-il ?; Environ trente-cinq degrés Celsius.; Ah bon ? Ici il fait froid. Il fait moins dix.

Activity B

1 a; 2 a; 3 b; 4 b

Activity C

1 d; 2 e; 3 b; 4 c; 5 a

Lesson 3

Activity A

Order may vary. Possible order:

Quelle température fait-il ?   Quel temps fait-il ?
35°C   Il fait chaud.
6°C   Il fait mauvais.
32°F   Il fait froid.

Activity B 1 b; 2 d; 3 a; 4 c

Activity C 1 a; 2 a; 3 b

Lesson 4

Activity A

1 la belle fille; 2 le petit chat; 3 la voiture rouge; 4 le livre américain; 5 la table ronde

Activity B 1 a; 2 a; 3 b; 4 a

Your Turn

Answers will vary.

Lesson 5

Activity A

activités en été: jouer au football, nager, courir, voyager
vêtements d'hiver: blouson, écharpe, gants, bottes

Activity B

1 plays soccer; 2 summer and winter; 3 winter; 4 Canada, 33

Lesson 6

Activity A

Answers will vary. Either *C'est ennuyant* or *C'est amusant* is acceptable.

Activity B

1 Qu'est-ce que vous faites ?; 2 Qu'est-ce que vous faites d'habitude ?; 3 D'habitude, en hiver je fais...; 4 Vous avez raison.

Your Turn Answers will vary.

Lesson 7

Activity A 1 les bottes; 2 les gants; 3 le chapeau

Activity B 1 l'automne; 2 le printemps; 3 l'hiver; 4 l'été

Activity C

1 un chapeau; 2 un blouson; 3 les sandales; 4 les gants

Lesson 8

Activity A 1 Marie se lave.; 2 Nous nous habillons.; 3 Tu te réveilles.; 4 Ils se rasent.

Activity B

1 Ils se marient.; 2 Ils s'embrassent.; 3 Elles se parlent.; 4 Ils se téléphonent.

Review

Activity A 1 b; 2 a; 3 b; 4 b; 5 a

Activity B

1 le chat gris; 2 la belle maison; 3 un bon travail; 4 un homme africain; 5 une jeune fille

Activity C 1 Il neige.; 2 Il fait froid.; 3 Il y a du vent.

Activity D

```
S O L E I L  Z S  C  S H K W Y  J
X Ç L A C H A Q  H  I V E R  V  V
E H H R W K M Q  A  Z K W X  P  L
H D A N J V R  A  U  T O M N E  J
Q P Y C X Q Z M  D  D Y D P Y  Ç
F D S L A P R I M A V É R A  V
X D O B M N A B R Z E K P E  E
Q A L F L M S O L E A D O I  N
F  P  R I N T E M P S  A T U R  T
P L Z Z Q G A L Q A W P E H  R
U U S T A C A L I D O D L L  F
A I J U G A R È G  F R O I D  W
B  E  V F  É  R H V R E P J U O  D
S Q W R  T  P K A P P J R N Y  U
T E M P  É  R A T U R E  L Q X N
```

Challenge

Answers will vary.

Unit 7 Lesson 1

Activity A

1 c; 2 b; 3 b

Activity B

1a; 2 b; 3 a

Lesson 2

Activity A

1 a; 2 a; 3 b; 4 a

Activity B

1 Je cherche une robe.; 2 Je cherche une chemise moyenne.;
3 Cette chemise est trop large.; 4 Je cherche une taille petite.

Lesson 3

Activity A

1 le tee-shirt; 2 le pantalon; 3 la robe; 4 le chemisier; 5 la jupe

Activity B

1 a; 2 a; 3 a; 4 a

Lesson 4

Activity A

1 m'habille; 2 met; 3 met; 4 portes

Activity B

1 mettez; 2 mets; 3 mets; 4 mettons; 5 mettent

Your Turn

je	m'	habille
tu	t'	habilles
il/elle	s'	habille
nous	nous	habillons
vous	vous	habillez
ils/elles	s'	habillent

Lesson 5

Activity A

1 a; 2 b; 3 a; 4 b

Activity B

1 a; 2 b; 3 b; 4 a

Lesson 6

Activity A

1 Acceptez-vous les cartes de crédit ?; 2 Combien coûte cette
jupe ?; 3 Acceptez-vous les chèques ?; 4 Je paierai par carte de
crédit.; 5 Combien coûte ce pantalon ?

Activity B

1 chère; 2 chère; 3 bon marché; 4 bon marché

Lesson 7

Activity A

1 chèques; 2 carte de crédit; 3 reçu; 4 argent

Activity B

J'ai 500 euros en **espèces** dans mon portefeuille. J'ai aussi une
carte de crédit. Je vais acheter beaucoup de vêtements parce
qu'il n'y a pas de **taxe**.

Lesson 8

Activity A

1 plus que; 2 moins que; 3 plus que; 4 moins que

Activity B

1 Quelqu'un; 2 Personne; 3 Quelques; 4 quelque chose

Review

Activity A

1 porte; 2 mettent; 3 portons; 4 s'habille

Challenge

je	mets
tu	mets
il/elle	met
nous	mettons
vous	mettez
ils/elles	mettent

Activity B

1 La chemise coûte moins que la jupe. La jupe coûte plus que
la chemise; 2 Le chemisier coûte moins que la robe. La robe
coûte plus que le chemisier.; 3 Le manteau coûte plus que les
chaussures. Les chaussures coûte moins que le manteau.; 4 Le
pantalon coûte moins que la cravate. La cravate coûte plus que le
pantalon.

Activity C

Unit 8 Lesson 1

Activity A

1 to arrive; 2 to take; 3 to walk

Activity B

1 la place du Parvis Notre-Dame; 2 à l'office de tourisme; 3 l'autobus ou le métro; 4 Elle veut voir la bibliothèque et les vieilles églises.

Lesson 2

Activity A

1 la bibliothèque; 2 la station de métro; 3 l'école; 4 l'église; 5 la gare routière; 6 l'arrêt d'autobus; 7 la poste; 8 le supermarché

Activity B

1 b; 2 b; 3 a; 4 b

Lesson 3

Activity A

1 Je veux prendre l'autobus. Où est l'arrêt d'autobus ?; 2 Je veux prendre le train. Où est la gare routière ?; 3 Je veux prendre le métro. Où est la station de métro ?

Activity B

1 Où est la gare routière ?; 2 Où est la station de métro ?; 3 La gare routière est près de l'école.; 4 Achetons une carte.

Activity C

1 Tu prends l'autobus à l'église.; 2 L'arrêt d'autobus est derrière la poste.

Your Turn

Excusez-moi. Où est l'arrêt d'autobus ? Comment vais-je à l'arrêt d'autobus ? Merci beaucoup !

Lesson 4

Activity A

1 vont; 2 va; 3 allons; 4 vas

Activity B

1 Allez; 2 vais; 3 vont; 4 allez

Activity C

1 Ils vont au supermarché.; 2 Nous allons à la station de métro.; 3 Elles vont à l'école.; 4 Vous allez à l'église.

Lesson 5

Activity A

1 b; 2 a; 3 a; 4 a

Activity B

22h; 14h

Lesson 6

Activity A

1 a; 2 a; 3 b; 4 b

Activity B

1 b; 2 d; 3 e; 4 c; 5 a

Lesson 7

Activity A

1 Le vol part à douze heures et demie.; 2 Quelle est la porte des départs ?; 3 Quelle est la porte des arrivées ?; 4 L'avion arrive à dix-sept heures.

Activity B

1 a; 2 a; 3 b

Activity C

1 Le vol part à dix-sept heures.; 2 Le vol pour Strasbourg part à dix-sept heures vingt.

Your Turn

Le prochain vol pour Paris, vol un-six-neuf-neuf, part à dix heures vingt-trois minutes. Le vol arrive à treize heures et demi.

Lesson 8

Activity A

1 connais; 2 connais; 3 connaissons; 4 connaissez

Activity B

1 Je le prends.; 2 Elle l'étudie.; 3 Tu la connais.; 4 Elles les prennent.

Your Turn

Answers will vary.

Review

Activity A

Chère Claire, Ma mère est moi sommes à Montréal. Demain, nous partons pour la ville de Québec. Tu **connais** Québec ? Je le **connais** bien. Ensuite, nous **allons** à Halifax. Est-ce que tu **connais** Halifax ? Bises, Tristan

Activity B

Mon voyage à Lyon. **Je vais** à Lyon en France. **Mon vol part à** 8h du matin. J'arrive **à l'aéroport** à 6h du matin. C'est si tôt ! J'ai mon **billet**, ma **bagage** et mon **passeport**. J'arrive à Lyon à 10h du matin et je cherche **un autobus** pour aller à l'hôtel. L'hôtel est **près de** la Place Bellecour. Je le connais. Il est **derrière une église**. Demain, **je veux prendre le métro** à l'Opéra National. J'ai besoin d'un ticket de métro. Ah, je l'ai.

Activity C

Auguste	Où est la poste ?
Véronique	**Achetons** une carte.
Auguste	Regardons le carte. La poste est **à droite de la** bibliothèque.
Véronique	Oui, est c'est aussi **derrière le supermarché.**
Auguste	C'est **l'arrêt d'autobus.**
Véronique	Oui. **Prenons** le bus ici.

Challenge

je sais; tu sais; il/elle sait; nous savons; vous savez; ils/elles savent

Unit 9 Lesson 1

Activity A 1 a; 2 b; 3 b; 4 a

Activity B 1 travaille; 2 a écrit; 3 culture; 4 commencera

Lesson 2

Activity A salle de classe; Le professeur; étudiants; journaliste; journal; magazine; étudiante

Activity B
a. la salle de classe; b. l'étudiant; c. le professeur
a. le bureau; b. le journaliste; c. la journaliste

Lesson 3

Activity A 1 professeur; 2 journaliste; 3 Je veux être journaliste.; 4 Je veux être professeur.

Activity B
1 Qu'est-ce que vous voulez faire ?; 2 Je veux être professeur.; 3 Quel est votre profession ?; 4 Je suis journaliste.

Your Turn

Answers may vary. Possible answers:
Bonjour, je m'appelle Devon. Je suis journaliste. Quelle est votre profession ? Je veux être artiste.

Lesson 4

Activity A 1 as travaillé; 2 a vendu; 3 ai fini; 4 avons travaillé

Activity B
1 J'ai travaillé au bureau.; 2 Vous avez vendu des livres de français.; 3 Elle a habité en France.; 4 Tu a mangé une salade.; 5 Elle a entendu la question.; 6 Marie et moi avons oublié de fermer la porte.

Lesson 5

Activity A
1 a proofreader; 2 four years; 3 Crédit Lyonnais; 4 Libération; 5 Le Monde

Activity B 1 desired position; 2 desired salary

Lesson 6

Activity A 1 c; 2 c; 3 b; 4 b

Activity B

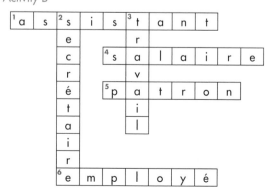

Your Turn
Answers will vary.

Lesson 7

Activity A

Answers will vary.

Activity B
1 Pourquoi désirez-vous être journaliste ?; 2 J'aime aider.; 3 Pendant combien de temps y avez-vous travaillé ?; 4 J'y ai travaillé pendant deux ans.

Lesson 8

Activity A

1 étudieras; 2 travaillerai; 3 écriront, 4 travaillerons

Activity B

1 J'étudierai le chinois.; 2 J'aiderai ma famille.; 3 Je rendrai visite à mes cousins.; 4 Je lirai un livre de Proust.; 5 Je corrigerai ma thèse.; 6 Je voyagerai une fois par mois.

Review

Activity A

¹é							²s				
t							e				
u							e				
³d	i	⁵f	f	i	c	i	l	e			
i		a			r						
a		c			é						
n		i			t						
t		l			a						
		e			i						
					r						
⁵p	r	o	f	e	s	s	e	u	r		

Activity B
1 Quand est-ce qu'elles travailleront ?; 2 Quand est-ce que tu as fini le livre ?; 3 Quand est-ce qu'elle vendra plus de livres ?

Activity C

Answers will vary. Possible answers:
1 Marie travaillera au bureau demain.; 2 J'ai vendu le DVD hier.; 3 Quand est-ce qu'elle visitera le Royaume-Uni ?; 4 Quand est-ce que nous avons mangé une pizza ?

Activity D

1 Quel est ton travail ?; 2 Pour qui est-ce que tu travailles ?; 3 Quel salaire souhaites-tu ?; 4 Quand est-ce qu'ils finiront le livre ?

Challenge
dur; souhaiter

Unit 10 Lesson 1

Activity A

1 b; 2 a; 3 b; 4 b

Activity B

1 Oui, il peut s'aider.; 2 Il ne veut pas ramasser ses vêtements.; 3 Il veut ranger le placard.; 4 Ils peuvent nettoyer et repeindre ensemble.

Lesson 2

Activity A

Answers will vary. Possible answers:

Ami Est-ce que tu habites dans une maison ou un appartement ?
Moi J'habite dans un appartement.
Ami Combien de pièces y a-t-il ?
Moi Il y a quatre pièces.
Ami Quelles sont les pièces les plus grandes ?
Moi Il y a la/les chambre(s), la salle à manger, la cuisine et la salle de séjour.

Activity B

1 la salle de séjour; 2 la cuisine; 3 la chambre; 4 la salle de bain; 5 la salle à manger; 6 le placard

Lesson 3

Activity A

1 Peux-tu m'aider ?; 2 Non, je ne peux pas t'aider.; 3 Qu'est-ce que tu veux que je fasse ?; 4 Tout de suite.

Activity B

1 Peux-tu m'aider ?; 2 Oui, je peux t'aider. Qu'est-ce que tu veux que je fasse ?; 3 Ramasse les vêtements.; 4 Tout de suite.

Lesson 4

Activity A

1 peut; 2 peut; 3 peuvent; 4 peut

Activity B

Ramassez les vêtements !; Peignez la chambre !; Organisez le placard !; Nettoyez le sol !

Lesson 5

Activity A 1 a; 2 b; 3 a; 4 b

Activity B

1 Chantal a passé une bonne semaine.; 2 Le concert a été très bien.; 3 Elle est allée en boîte.; 4 Elle est allée avec ton copain.

Activity C

1 Avant-hier, mes amis et moi sommes allés à un concert de rock.; 2 Hier, ma mère et moi sommes allées dans un magasin pour acheter des vêtements.; 3 Ensuite, je suis allée en boîte avec mon copain et nous avons dansé toute la nuit.

Lesson 6

Activity A 1 le bar; 2 le cinéma; 3 le théâtre; 4 le concert

Activity B

1 hier; 2 avant-hier; 3 la semaine dernière; 4 hier soir

Activity C

Lesson 7

Activity A

1 Qu'est-ce que tu as fait la semaine dernière ?; 2 Qu'est-ce que tu veux faire ?; 3 Je veux sortir.; 4 Je veux rester à la maison.

Activity B

1 **Édouard** Qu'est-ce que tu veux faire ce soir ?
2 **Manon** Je veux rester à la maison ce soir.
3 **Édouard** Mais moi, je ne veux pas rester à la maison. Veux-tu aller danser ?
4 **Manon** Je suis allée danser avec mes amies hier.
5 **Édouard** Veux-tu aller au cinéma?
6 **Manon** Nous sommes allés au cinéma hier soir.
7 **Édouard** Nous restons donc à la maison ce soir.
Édouard reste à la maison.

Your Turn Answers will vary.

Lesson 8

Activity A 1 a; 2 b; 3 b; 4 b

Activity B 1 suis allé(e); 2 es allé(e); 3 est allé; 4 sommes allé(e)s; 5 sont allés; 6 sont allé(e)s

Activity C 1 I went to my mother's house last night.; 2 You went to work yesterday.; 3 He went to school this morning.; 4 We went to the concert the day before yesterday.; 5 They went to the movies last Monday.; 6 My friends went to Brussels last year.

Your Turn Answers will vary.

Review

Activity A 1 toilette; 2 film; 3 danser; 4 peindre; 5 cuisine

Activity B 1 b; 2 a; 3 b; 4 a

Activity C 1 Vous êtes allés/allées à l'école.; 2 Où est-ce que tu es allé/allée ?; 3 Nous sommes allés/allées à la bibliothèque.; 4 Je suis allé/allée au restaurant.

Activity D 1 Aide-moi nettoyer !; 2 Aidez-la !; 3 Ramasses ses vêtements !; 4 Ramassez ce livre !

Challenge 1 Peux-tu m'aider à nettoyer ?; 2 Pouvez-vous s'aider ? 3 Peux-tu ramasser ses vêtements ? 4 Pouvez-vous ramasser ce livre ?

Unit 11 Lesson 1

Activity A

1 a; 2 b; 3 b; 4 b

Activity B

1 a; 2 b; 3 a

Lesson 2

Activity A

1 la natation; 2 le football; 3 le tennis; 4 le cyclisme

Activity B

1 le gymnase; 2 poids; 3 gras; 4 mince, saine; 5 stressé(e);
6 malade

Activity C

1 b; 2 a; 3 a; 4 b

Lesson 3

Activity A

1 Je suis en bonne santé.; 2 Je veux être en forme.; 3 Je suis
malade.; 4 Je veux perdre du poids.

Activity B

1 a; 2 a; 3 b; 4 b; 5 a

Lesson 4

Activity A

1 Il va écrire.; 2 Je vais danser.; 3 Elles vont étudier.; 4 Nous
allons jouer.; 5 Tu vas manger.; 6 Elle va courir.

Activity B

1 Quand est-ce que tu vas regarder le film ?; 2. Quand est-ce
qu'elle va me téléphoner ?; 3 Quand est-ce que nous allons
habiter à Bruges ?; 4 Quand est-ce que Fabien va te téléphoner ?;
5 Quand est-ce que Émille et Arnaud vont boire de la bière ?; 6
Quand est-ce que vous allez manger du coq au vin ?

Your Turn

1 Il va pleuvoir.; 2 Ils vont manger.; 3 Il va jouer.; 4 Elle va écrire.

Lesson 5

Activity A

1 a; 2 a; 3 b; 4 a; 5 b

Activity B

1 b; 2 b; 3 a; 4 b; 5 a

Activity C

Les deux médicaments soignent la fièvre. Le médicament contre la
toux soigne le mal de gorge, et la contre le rhume soigne le mal
de tête et de gorge.

Lesson 6

Activity A

1 b; 2 b; 3 b; 4 a; 5 a

Activity B

1. Il a mal au ventre.; 2 Elle a le rhume.; 3 Il a mal de tête.;
4 Elle a rage de dent.

Your Turn

Answers will vary. Possible answers:
Tu as mal de gorge. Je vais vous donner une ordonnance.

Lesson 7

Activity A

Answers will vary. Possible answers:
J'ai mal au ventre, et aussi j'ai de la fièvre. J'ai besoin de
médicament.

Activity B

Answers may vary. Possible answers:
Réné Cartier a mal au ventre. Il a de la fièvre aussi. Il doit voir un
médecin tout de suite.

Activity C

1 main; 2 dos; 3 pied; 4 bras

Lesson 8

Activity A

Answers will vary.

Activity B

1 Je suis parfois malade.; 2 Je vais au gymnase toujours.;
3 D'habitude, je suis en bonne santé.; 4 Je joue au tennis une
fois par semaine.; 5 Je ne prends jamais le médicament.

Activity C

1 Vas-tu aller au gymnase toujours le mardi ?;
2 Est-ce que Françoise joue au football toutes les semaines ?

Your Turn

Answers will vary.

Review

Activity A

Je me sens bon.; Je suis en bonne santé.; Je ne vais pas aller
chez le dentiste.; Je n'ai pas mal au ventre.; Je veux aller chez le
médecin.

Activity B

1 J'ai mal de tête.; 2 Je vais habiter en France.; 3 Je cours deux
fois par semaine.; 4 Thierry va courir au parc.; 5 Nous allons
manger les sandwiches.; 6 J'ai mal au pied.

Activity C

1 cyclisme; 2 tennis; 3 mal de tête; 4 médicament; 5 fièvre;
6 dentiste

Challenge

Answers will vary.

Interior

p. 8: (TL) © Oraneg Line Media 2008/Shutterstock, Inc., (TR) © Jason Stitt 2008/ Shutterstock, Inc., (RC) © Jason Stitt 2008/Shutterstock, Inc., (BR) © Edyta Pawlowska 2008/Shutterstock, Inc.; p. 9: (TR) © Yuri Arcurs 2008/Shutterstock, Inc., (TRC) © Dmitriy Shironosov 2008/Shutterstock, Inc., (BRC) © 2008 Jupiter Images, Inc., (BR) © 2008 Jupiter Images, Inc.; p. 10: (TL) © Raia 2008/Shutterstock, Inc., (TR) © ZTS 2008/Shutterstock, Inc., (B, Bkgrd) © Lars Christensen 2008/ Shutterstock, Inc., (BL, Inset) © Sean Nel 2008/Shutterstock, Inc., (BLC, Inset) © Elena Elisseeva 2008/Shutterstock, Inc., (BRC, Inset) © movit 2008/Shutterstock, Inc., (BR, Inset) © Daniel Leppens 2008/Shutterstock, Inc.; p. 11: (TL) © Lisa F. Young 2008/ Shutterstock, Inc., (TRC) © 2008 Jupiter Images, Inc., (TR) © 2008 Jupiter Images, Inc., (CL) © Bobby Deal 2008/Shutterstock, Inc., (CLC) © 2008 Jupiter Images, Inc., (CRC) © Yuri Arcurs 2008/Shutterstock, Inc., (CR) © 2008 Jupiter Images, Inc., (BLL) © 2008 Jupiter Images, Inc., (BL) © Yuri Arcurs 2008/Shutterstock, Inc., (BLC) © Konstantynov 2008/Shutterstock, Inc., (BR) © Andresr 2008/Shutterstock, Inc.; p. 13: (TL) © Sandra G 2008/Shutterstock, Inc., (TRC) © Lukas Wroblewski 2008/ Shutterstock, Inc., (TR) © Pilar Echevarria 2008/Shutterstock, Inc., (CRT) © Robyn Mackenzie 2008/Shutterstock, Inc., (CRB) © Edyta Pawlowska 2008/Shutterstock, Inc., (BL) © 2008 Jupiter Images, Inc., (BLT) © photobank.ch 2008/Shutterstock, Inc., (BLC) © Supri Suharjoto 2008/Shutterstock, Inc., (BLB) © Niels Quist 2008/ Shutterstock, Inc., (BRC) © Daniel Wiedemann 2008/Shutterstock, Inc.; p. 14: © Vladislav Gurfinkel 2008/Shutterstock, Inc.; p. 15: (T) © Yuri Arcurs 2008/ Shutterstock, Inc., (BL) © Andre Nantel 2008/Shutterstock, Inc., (BR) © Dmitriy Shironosov 2008/Shutterstock, Inc.; p. 16: © St. Nick 2008/Shutterstock, Inc.; p. 17: (TL, Inset) © Pavel Sazonov 2008/Shutterstock, Inc., (TLC, Inset) © Alfgar 2008/ Shutterstock, Inc., (TRC, Inset) © Carmen Ruiz 2008/Shutterstock, Inc., (TR, Inset) © 2008 Jupiter Images, Inc., (C) © Doug Raphael 2008/Shutterstock, Inc., (BL, Inset) © Galina Barskaya 2008/Shutterstock, Inc., (BLC, Inset) © Scott A. Frangos 2008/ Shutterstock, Inc., (BRC, Inset) © Jacek Chabraszewski 2008/Shutterstock, Inc., (BR, Inset) © Elena Elisseeva 2008/Shutterstock, Inc., (BR) © Kiselev Andrey Valerevich 2008/Shutterstock, Inc.; p. 18: (TLL) © Photobank.ch 2008/Shutterstock, Inc., (TLC) © Yuri Arcurs 2008/Shutterstock, Inc., (TLR) © vgstudio 2008/Shutterstock, Inc., (TR, Bkgrd) © Iofoto 2008/Shutterstock, Inc., (TR, Inset) © Stacy Barnett 2008/ Shutterstock, Inc., (CLL) © BESTWEB 2008/Shutterstock, Inc., (CLC) © Lexx 2008/ Shutterstock, Inc., (CLR) © Alexey Nikolaew 2008/Shutterstock, Inc., (LL, Inset) © Kristian Sekulic 2008/Shutterstock, Inc., (LC, Inset) © Sandy Maya Matzen 2008/ Shutterstock, Inc., (C, Inset) © Galina Barskaya 2008/Shutterstock, Inc., (R, Bkgrd) © Arthur Eugene Preston 2008/Shutterstock, Inc., (RC, Inset) © Rob Wilson 2008/ Shutterstock, Inc., (RR, Inset) © Luminis 2008/Shutterstock, Inc.,(BLL) © Vladimir Melnik 2008/Shutterstock, Inc., (BLC) © Denise Kappa 2008/Shutterstock, Inc., (BLR) © MalibuBooks 2008/Shutterstock, Inc., (BCL) © fckncg 2008/Shutterstock, Inc., (BCR) © Hannu Lilvaar 2008/Shutterstock, Inc., (B) © James Steidl 2008/ Shutterstock, Inc.; p. 19: (T) © Nagy-Bagoly Arpad 2008/Shutterstock, Inc., (TR) © Velychko 2008/Shutterstock, Inc. (L) © Yuri Arcurs 2008/Shutterstock, Inc., (CL) © Dmitriy Shironosov 2008/Shutterstock, Inc., (CRL) © Erik Lam 2008/Shutterstock, Inc., (CRC) © Suponev Vladimir Mihajlovich 2008/Shutterstock, Inc., (CRR) © mlorenz 2008/Shutterstock, Inc., (B) © Vaclav Volrab 2008/Shutterstock, Inc., (BR) © Doug Raphael 2008/Shutterstock, Inc.; p. 20: (TL) © Andresr 2008/Shutterstock, Inc., (TR) © Ustyujanin 2008/Shutterstock, Inc., (CLT) © Andrey Armyagov 2008/ Shutterstock, Inc., (CLB) © Rafa Irusta 2008/Shutterstock, Inc., (CRL) © Margo Harrison 2008/Shutterstock, Inc., (CR) © Yuri Arcurs 2008/Shutterstock, Inc., (CRR) © Hannu Lilvaar 2008/Shutterstock, Inc., (CRB) © melkerw 2008/Shutterstock, Inc., (BL) © BESTWEB 2008/Shutterstock, Inc., (BLC) © ene 2008/Shutterstock, Inc., (BR) © Kiselev Andrey Valerevich 2008/Shutterstock, Inc.; p. 21: © Sam DCruz 2008/ Shutterstock, Inc.; p. 22: (TL) © Scott Waldron 2008/Shutterstock, Inc., (BR) © Liv Friis-larsen 2008/Shutterstock, Inc.; p. 23: (TL) © 2008 Jupiter Images, Inc., (TRC) © J2008 upiter Images, Inc., (TR) © J2008 upiter Images, Inc., (C) © Aga_Rafi 2008/ Shutterstock, Inc., (BL) © Andy Lim 2008/Shutterstock, Inc., (BRC) © J2008 upiter Images, Inc., (BR) © J2008 upiter Images, Inc.; p. 24: (TL) © 2008 Jupiter Images, Inc., (TR) © Monkey Business Images 2008/Shutterstock, Inc., (RC) © Andrejs Pidjass 2008/Shutterstock, Inc., (BR) © Donna Heatfield 2008/Shutterstock, Inc.; p. 25: (TL) © Nick Stubbs 2008/Shutterstock, Inc., (TLC) © Daniela Mangiuca 2008/ Shutterstock, Inc., (LCL) © Tomasz Pietryszek 2008/Shutterstock, Inc., (LC) © Philip Date 2008/Shutterstock, Inc., (LCR) © Michael Ransburg 2008/Shutterstock, Inc., (BL) © Raia 2008/Shutterstock, Inc.; p. 26: (T, Bkgrd) © yurok 2008/Shutterstock, Inc., (T, Inset) © 2008 Jupiter Images, Inc., (L, Inset) © Stephen Mcsweeny 2008/ Shutterstock, Inc., (C, Inset) © Michelle Marsan 2008/Shutterstock, Inc., (CR) © MaxFX 2008/Shutterstock, Inc., (R, Inset) © Tatiana Strelkova 2008/Shutterstock, Inc., (R) © Steve Luker 2008/Shutterstock, Inc., (BC) © MaxFX 2008/Shutterstock, Inc., (BRC) © Steve Luker 2008/Shutterstock, Inc., (BR) © Bart Everett 2008/ Shutterstock, Inc.; p. 27: (TL) © Andresr 2008/Shutterstock, Inc., (TR) © laurent hamels 2008/Shutterstock, Inc., (BR) © Fatini Zulnaidi 2008/Shutterstock, Inc.; p. 28: (TL) © Konstantin Remizov 2008/Shutterstock, Inc., (BL) © Leo Blanchette 2008/ Shutterstock, Inc.; p. 29: (TRC) © 2008 Jupiter Images, Inc., (TR) © Dmitriy Shironosov 2008/Shutterstock, Inc., (LC) © 2008 Jupiter Images, Inc., (RC) © Larisa Lofitskaya 2008/Shutterstock, Inc., (BL) © Marina Krasnorutskaya 2008/ Shutterstock, Inc., (BRC) © Carlo Dapino 2008/Shutterstock, Inc., (BR) © as-foto 2008/Shutterstock, Inc.; p. 30: (T) © Rafa Irusta 2008/Shutterstock, Inc., (TL) © Orange Line Media 2008/Shutterstock, Inc., (TLC) © 2008 Jupiter Images, Inc., ., (TRC) © Stephen Coburn 2008/Shutterstock, Inc., (TR) © Gina Sanders 2008/ Shutterstock, Inc., (CL) © tinatka 2008/Shutterstock, Inc., (CR) © Elena Ray 2008/ Shutterstock, Inc., (BL) © George Dolgikh 2008/Shutterstock, Inc., (BC) © David Hyde 2008/Shutterstock, Inc., (BRC) © J. Helgason 2008/Shutterstock, Inc., (BR) © 2happy 2008/Shutterstock, Inc.; p. 32: (TR) © Jakez 2008/Shutterstock, Inc., (B) © Phil Date 2008/Shutterstock, Inc.; p. 33: (T) © Dmitriy Shironosov 2008/ Shutterstock, Inc., (TRC) © Simone van den Berg 2008/Shutterstock, Inc., (TR) © 2008 Jupiter Images, Inc., (BLC) © Tomasz Trojanowski 2008/Shutterstock, Inc., (BR) © Stephen Mcsweeny 2008/Shutterstock, Inc.; p. 34: (BL) © Mike Flippo 2008/ Shutterstock, Inc., (BR) © Pakhnyushcha 2008/Shutterstock, Inc.; p. 35: (T) © Christian Wheatley 2008/Shutterstock, Inc., (TL) © Simon Krzic 2008/Shutterstock, Inc., (TLC) © Edyta Pawlowska 2008/Shutterstock, Inc., (TC) © MWProductions 2008/Shutterstock, Inc., (TRC) © Dusaleev Viatcheslav 2008/Shutterstock, Inc., (TR) © Olga Lyubkina 2008/Shutterstock, Inc.; p. 36: (Bkgrd) © khz 2008/Shutterstock, Inc., (CL) © Andresr 2008/Shutterstock, Inc., (CR) © T-Design 2008/Shutterstock, Inc., (B) © Ivan Jelisavic 2008/Shutterstock, Inc., (BL) © Jason Stitt 2008/ Shutterstock, Inc., (BR) © Dimitrije Paunovic 2008/Shutterstock, Inc.; p. 37: (TL) © Vibrant Image Studio 2008/Shutterstock, Inc., (TRC) © Jeanne Hatch 2008/ Shutterstock, Inc., (TR) © Ersler Dmitry 2008/Shutterstock, Inc., (L) © iofoto 2008/ Shutterstock, Inc., (CL) © iofoto 2008/Shutterstock, Inc., (BL) © iofoto 2008/ Shutterstock, Inc., (BRC) © Jaren Jai Wicklund 2008/Shutterstock, Inc., (BR) © Adam Borkowski 2008/Shutterstock, Inc.; p. 38: (TL) © Lisa F. Young 2008/Shutterstock, Inc., (TRC) © Martin Valigursky 2008/Shutterstock, Inc., (TR) © Monkey Business Images 2008/Shutterstock, Inc., (R) © Sonya Etchison 2008/Shutterstock, Inc., (RCT) © Vibrant Image Studio 2008/Shutterstock, Inc., (RCB) © Monkey Business Images 2008/Shutterstock, Inc., (BRC) © Denise Kappa 2008/Shutterstock, Inc., (BR) © Monkey Business Images 2008/Shutterstock, Inc.; p. 39: (TL) © Evgeny V. Kan 2008/Shutterstock, Inc., (TR) © Carme Balcells 2008/Shutterstock, Inc., (L) © Sandra G 2008/Shutterstock, Inc., (LC) © Kurhan 2008/Shutterstock, Inc., (RC) © Simon Krzic 2008/Shutterstock, Inc., (R) © Carme Balcells 2008/Shutterstock, Inc., (BL) © Lexx 2008/Shutterstock, Inc., (C) © Konstantin Sutyagin 2008/Shutterstock, Inc., (BLC) © Allgord 2008/Shutterstock, Inc., (BRC) © Sandra G 2008/Shutterstock, Inc., (BR) © Andriy Goncharenko 2008/Shutterstock, Inc., (BBL) © Dagmara Ponikiewska 2008/Shutterstock, Inc., (BBR) © KSR 2008/Shutterstock, Inc.; p. 40: (TL) © Lisa F. Young 2008/Shutterstock, Inc., (B) © Elena Ray 2008/Shutterstock, Inc., (BL) © Najin 2008/Shutterstock, Inc., (BR) © Elena Ray 2008/Shutterstock, Inc.; p. 41: (TL) © Losevsky Pavel 2008/Shutterstock, Inc., (TR) © Ustyujanin 2008/ Shutterstock, Inc., (B) © Elena Ray 2008/Shutterstock, Inc., (BL) © Elena Ray 2008/ Shutterstock, Inc., (BLC) © Vitezslav Halamka 2008/Shutterstock, Inc., (BRC) © Vitezslav Halamka 2008/Shutterstock, Inc., (BR) © Robin Mackenzie 2008/ Shutterstock, Inc.; p. 42: (TL) © Serghei Starus 2008/Shutterstock, Inc., (TLC) © Jaimie Duplass 2008/Shutterstock, Inc., (BL) © Rui Vale de Sousa 2008/Shutterstock, Inc., (BLC) © Steve Snowden 2008/Shutterstock, Inc., (BR) © 2008 Jupiter Images, Inc.; p. 43: (TL) © Monkey Business Images 2008/Shutterstock, Inc., (TR) © Sandra G 2008/Shutterstock, Inc., (BL) © Monkey Business Images 2008/Shutterstock, Inc., (BR) © Konstantin Sutyagin 2008/Shutterstock, Inc.; p. 44: (TL) © Sergey Rusakov 2008/Shutterstock, Inc., (TLC) © Joe Gough 2008/Shutterstock, Inc., (TRC) © Valentyn Volkov 2008/Shutterstock, Inc., (TR) © RexRover 2008/Shutterstock, Inc., (CR) © Rudchenko Liliia 2008/Shutterstock, Inc., (R) © imageZebra 2008/ Shutterstock, Inc., (BL) © Ljupco Smokovski 2008/Shutterstock, Inc., (BLC) © Peter Polak 2008/Shutterstock, Inc., (BRC) © Edyta Pawlowska 2008/Shutterstock, Inc., (BR) © Edyta Pawlowska 2008/Shutterstock, Inc.; p. 45: (TL) © Edyta Pawlowska 2008/Shutterstock, Inc., (TRC) © Dusan Zidar 2008/Shutterstock, Inc., (TR) © Supri Suharjoto 2008/Shutterstock, Inc., (R) © Edw 2008/Shutterstock, Inc., (RC) © Monkey Business Images 2008/Shutterstock, Inc., (BLC) © JanP 2008/Shutterstock, Inc., (BR) © 2008 Jupiter Images, Inc.; p. 46: (TL) © Ana Blazic 2008/Shutterstock, Inc., (TR) © Alexander Shalamov 2008/Shutterstock, Inc., (R) © Phil Date 2008/ Shutterstock, Inc., (BL) © Galina Barskaya 2008/Shutterstock, Inc., (BR) © Dragan Trifunovic 2008/Shutterstock, Inc.; p. 47: (TL) © Steve Luker 2008/Shutterstock, Inc., (BL) © Andre Nantel 2008/Shutterstock, Inc.; p. 48: (TL) © 2008 Jupiter Images, Inc., (TLC) © Viktor1 2008/Shutterstock, Inc., (TRC) © Robyn Mackenzie 2008/ Shutterstock, Inc., (TR) © Joe Gough 2008/Shutterstock, Inc., (L) © Jackie Carvey 2008/Shutterstock, Inc., (LC) © Anna Nizami 2008/Shutterstock, Inc., (B) © Andrejs Pidjass 2008/Shutterstock, Inc., (BL) © Sarune Zurbaite 2008/Shutterstock, Inc., (BLC) © Bochkarev Photography 2008/Shutterstock, Inc., (BRC) © Liv Friis-Larsen 2008/Shutterstock, Inc., (BR) © Kheng Guan Toh 2008/Shutterstock, Inc.; p. 49: (TL) © Rene Jansa 2008/Shutterstock, Inc., (TRC) © Joe Gough 2008/Shutterstock, Inc., (TR) © Valentin Mosichev 2008/Shutterstock, Inc., (CR) © Olga Lyubkina 2008/ Shutterstock, Inc., (R) © Joe Gough 2008/Shutterstock, Inc., (BL) © 2008 Jupiter Images, Inc., (BRC) © Paul Maguire 2008/Shutterstock, Inc., (BR) © Viktor1 2008/ Shutterstock, Inc.; p. 50: (TL) © 2008 Jupiter Images, Inc., (BL) © Robyn Mackenzie 2008/Shutterstock, Inc., (BR) © Keith Wheatley 2008/Shutterstock, Inc.; p. 51: (TL) © Lisa F. Young 2008/Shutterstock, Inc., (BL) © David P. Smith 2008/Shutterstock, Inc., (BLC) © Dusan Zidar 2008/Shutterstock, Inc., (BRC) © David P. Smith 2008/